THE GOLDEN RULE IN LEADERSHIP

ALLIGNING PURPOSE FOR SUCCESS

Written By
Dr. Ty H. Wenglar, PhD

Dedication

To my beloved wife.

Cathy, you have been my rock, enduring the long hours and absences, managing our household, caring for our children with unwavering dedication, and ensuring our home was a place of peace and progress. Your ability to juggle countless responsibilities while being my steadfast supporter is nothing short of miraculous. I am forever grateful for your love, patience, and sacrifice.

Acknowledgments

To my parents, Buck and Lisa Wenglar and Sandi Richards, who planted the seeds of curiosity and love for learning in me. Thank you for teaching me the value of education and for being my constant source of motivation and encouragement.

In the loving memory of my grandmother, Myrtle "Totsie" Wenglar, whose support and belief in my potential were unwavering.

About The Author

Dr. Ty H. Wenglar is an accomplished construction executive and scholar in Organizational Leadership with extensive experience in multi-family development and construction. Renowned for his player-coach leadership style and a proactive, results-oriented mindset, Dr. Wenglar is actively involved in academic and community leadership roles. He has a passion for teaching, mentoring, and conducting research in leadership ethics and practices.

Dr. Wenglar's academic focus lies at the intersection of leadership ethics and organizational effectiveness, focusing on how foundational ethical principles like the Golden Rule influence leadership styles across different cultural and organizational contexts. His doctoral dissertation, "Exploring the Intersection of Ethical and Virtuous Leadership: An Analysis of Correlation and Interchangeability of Measurement Tools," investigates the measurable impact of ethical and virtuous leadership traits on organizational outcomes.

Additionally, Dr. Wenglar's research delves into the application of ethical principles in leadership, seeking to enhance both theoretical and practical understanding of how aligning organizational purposes with ethical leadership can foster environments of compassion and integrity. Through his extensive experience and academic contributions, Dr. Wenglar continues to inspire leaders to embrace ethical practices and create positive, lasting impacts in their organizations and communities.

Table of Contents

Introduction

The Golden Rule in Leadership

In a world that often prioritizes profit over people, the essence of true leadership can easily be overshadowed by short-term gains and transactional relationships. Yet, history and experience reveal that the most impactful leaders are those who understand and practice the Golden Rule: treating others as they wish to be treated. "The Golden Rule in Leadership: Aligning Purpose for Success" seeks to illuminate this timeless principle and demonstrate how it can serve as the cornerstone of effective leadership.

Gone are the days when a leader's success was solely measured by financial metrics and hierarchical dominance. Today, the most successful leaders are those who align their personal values and organizational objectives with a higher purpose, creating environments where trust, empathy, and mutual respect flourish. This book explores how leaders can integrate the Golden Rule into their daily practices, fostering workplaces that are not only productive but also genuinely fulfilling for everyone involved (Brown & Treviño, 2006).

The concept of the Golden Rule, often phrased as "treat others as you would like to be treated," is a universal principle that transcends cultural and religious boundaries. Its core message of empathy and reciprocity is evident in the teachings of many traditions around the world. In Christianity, the Golden Rule is encapsulated in Jesus' teaching: "Do unto others as you would have them do unto you" (Matthew 7:12, New International Version). This principle encourages followers to act with kindness and consideration, fostering a community built on mutual respect. In Islam, a similar notion is found in the Hadith: "None of you truly believes until he loves for his brother what he loves for himself" (Sahih Muslim, Book 1, Hadith 72). This emphasizes the importance of empathy and altruism, urging individuals to consider the welfare of others as integral to their own faith. Similarly, in

Judaism, the Torah teaches, "Love your neighbor as yourself" (Leviticus 19:18, New International Version), promoting a sense of shared humanity and collective responsibility. Hinduism also echoes this sentiment with the Mahabharata stating, "This is the sum of duty: do not do to others what would cause pain if done to you" (Mahabharata, 5:1517). Here, the focus is on avoiding harm and fostering harmony. Buddhism, with its emphasis on compassion and mindfulness, advises: "Hurt not others in ways that you yourself would find hurtful" (Udana-Varga 5:18). These diverse yet convergent teachings underscore the Golden Rule's universal applicability (Gensler, 2013).

In leadership, this principle can be a guiding light, helping leaders foster inclusive and harmonious work environments. By recognizing and respecting this shared ethical foundation, leaders can bridge cultural divides, align team purpose, and drive collective success. Understanding the Golden Rule's presence across cultures and religions enriches its application, encouraging leaders to embody empathy, fairness, and integrity in their pursuit of excellence (Johnson, 2022).

Through a combination of real-world examples, thought-provoking insights, and actionable strategies, this book will guide you on a journey to becoming a leader who inspires and motivates. Whether you are an executive, manager, or aspiring leader, the principles outlined here will help you build stronger teams, make more ethical decisions, and ultimately achieve sustainable success.

References

Brown, M. E., & Treviño, L. K. (2006). Ethical leadership: A review and future directions. *The Leadership Quarterly, 17*(6), 595-616.

Gensler, H. J. (2013). *Ethics and the Golden Rule*. Routledge.

Johnson, L. (2022). *Global ethics and the environment: A leadership approach*. Springer.

Kaptein, M. (2011). Understanding unethical behavior by unraveling ethical culture. *Human Relations, 64*(6), 843-869.

Treviño, L. K., & Nelson, K. A. (2014). *Managing business ethics: Straight talk about how to do it right* (6th ed.). Wiley.

Chapter 1

The Golden Rule Across Cultures and Religions

The concept of the Golden Rule, often phrased as "treat others as you would like to be treated," is a universal principle that transcends cultural and religious boundaries. Its core message of empathy and reciprocity is evident in the teachings of many traditions around the world. This chapter explores how the Golden Rule is articulated in various religious and cultural contexts, demonstrating its universal relevance and profound impact on leadership and organizational behavior.

Historical Perspectives on the Golden Rule

The Golden Rule is one of the oldest ethical principles known to humanity, appearing in various forms across ancient civilizations. Its simplicity and profound ethical implications have made it a cornerstone of moral teachings worldwide. In ancient Egypt, the principle was articulated as "Do for one who may do for you, that you may cause him thus to do" in "The Tale of the Eloquent Peasant" (circa 2000 BCE), emphasizing mutual respect and reciprocal behavior. This principle of reciprocity was deeply woven into the fabric of Egyptian society, reflecting the broader cultural value of *Ma'at* or cosmic order, which encompassed truth, justice, balance, and harmony (Johnson, 2017).

In ancient Greece, the philosopher Pittacus stated, "Do not to your neighbor what you would take ill from him." This precept was integral to Greek philosophy and was explored extensively by figures such as Socrates, Plato, and Aristotle, who linked it to concepts of justice, civic duty, and ethical leadership. Greek leaders were expected to personify these virtues, fostering a polis where the interests of the community were paramount

(Harrison, 2019).

Confucius, in ancient China, encapsulated the Golden Rule in the Analects: "What you do not wish for yourself, do not do to others" (circa 500 BCE). This principle underscores the importance of benevolence, propriety, and reciprocity in personal behavior and leadership. Confucian leadership is expected to demonstrate moral rectitude and to govern with compassion and wisdom, fostering a harmonious society (Lee, 2018).

Manifestation in Major Religions

Christianity

In Christianity, the Golden Rule is encapsulated in Jesus' teaching: "Do unto others as you would have them do unto you" (Matthew 7:12, New International Version). This principle encourages followers to act with kindness and consideration, fostering a community built on mutual respect. Jesus' teaching emphasizes empathy, urging believers to put themselves in others' shoes and act with compassion and integrity. This directive forms a foundational ethic that influences Christian leadership, promoting servant leadership where leaders prioritize the well-being and development of their followers (Miller, 2019).

Islam

In Islam, a similar notion is found in the Hadith: "None of you truly believes until he loves for his brother what he loves for himself" (Sahih Muslim, Book 1, Hadith 72). This emphasizes the importance of empathy and altruism, urging individuals to consider the welfare of others as integral to their own faith. Islamic leadership is characterized by justice (*adl*), consultation (*shura*), and community welfare, reflecting the comprehensive application of the Golden Rule. Leaders are expected to act with moral integrity, fairness, and concern for the well-being of their followers, embodying the ethical teachings of the Quran and the Hadith (Rahimi, 2021).

Judaism

In Judaism, the Torah teaches, "Love your neighbor as yourself" (Leviticus 19:18, New International Version), promoting a sense of shared humanity and collective responsibility. This principle is central to Jewish ethics, influencing leadership practices that emphasize fairness, integrity, and community welfare. Jewish leaders are encouraged to engage in practices that reflect the values of *tzedakah* (charity) and *tikkun olam* (repairing the world), advocating for and implementing policies that protect the vulnerable and promote equity and fairness within society (Solomon, 2017).

Hinduism

Hinduism echoes this sentiment with the Mahabharata stating, "This is the sum of duty: do not do to others what would cause pain if done to you" (Mahabharata, 5:1517). Here, the focus is on avoiding harm and fostering harmony. Hindu leaders are tasked with the dual responsibility of achieving personal spiritual growth and contributing to the welfare of society. This involves making decisions that align with ethical standards and contribute to the common good, ensuring that actions taken are beneficial for all stakeholders. The practice of the Golden Rule in Hindu leadership encourages an inclusive approach, where the needs and well-being of followers are placed at the forefront of all initiatives and policies (Klostermaier, 2018).

Buddhism

Buddhism, with its emphasis on compassion and mindfulness, advises: "Hurt not others in ways that you yourself would find hurtful" (Udana-Varga 5:18). This principle is integral to Buddhist teachings, guiding leaders to act with kindness and avoid causing harm. Buddhist leadership is characterized by compassion, mindfulness, and ethical conduct, promoting a holistic approach that considers the long-term impacts of their actions. Leaders are encouraged to create conditions that facilitate peace, understanding, and mutual respect among individuals (Thompson, 2020).

Philosophical Underpinnings and Universality

The philosophical underpinnings of the Golden Rule highlight its universal applicability and ethical significance. Philosophers such as Immanuel Kant have articulated similar principles in their ethical theories. Kant's Categorical Imperative, for instance, requires individuals to act according to maxims that can be universally applied, reflecting the essence of the Golden Rule (Gensler, 2013).

The universality of the Golden Rule is evident in its presence across diverse cultural and religious traditions. Despite variations in expression, the core message remains the same: treat others with the empathy and respect you wish to receive. This universal ethical guideline promotes social harmony, ethical behavior, and mutual respect, making it a foundational principle in leadership (Kapoor, 2020).

The Golden Rule as a Guiding Light in Leadership

In leadership, the Golden Rule can be a guiding light, helping leaders foster inclusive and harmonious work environments. By recognizing and respecting this shared ethical foundation, leaders can bridge cultural divides, align team purpose, and drive collective success. Understanding the Golden Rule's presence across cultures and religions enriches its application, encouraging leaders to embody empathy, fairness, and integrity in their pursuit of excellence (Treviño & Nelson, 2014).

Effective leaders who practice the Golden Rule create environments where trust, empathy, and mutual respect flourish. They align their personal values and organizational objectives with a higher purpose, fostering workplaces that are not only productive but also genuinely fulfilling for everyone involved. By treating employees with fairness and consideration, leaders inspire loyalty, enhance team cohesion, and drive organizational success (Johnson, 2022).

Real-World Applications and Benefits

Research in diverse organizational settings has demonstrated that leaders who practice the Golden Rule see marked improvements in teamwork, employee loyalty, and overall organizational performance. For instance, companies with leadership practices rooted in fairness and mutual respect report higher levels of innovation and employee satisfaction. Similarly, in the dynamic environments of start-ups and technology firms, leaders who employ the Golden Rule in managing their teams are more likely to foster a culture of innovation where creative ideas and risk-taking are encouraged (Gensler, 2013).

The Golden Rule's application in leadership extends beyond ethical behavior; it is a strategic tool for aligning organizational purposes with personal values. By integrating this principle into their leadership practices, leaders can enhance communication, improve conflict resolution, and foster a culture of ethical integrity and mutual respect. These practices are not just beneficial; they are essential in today's complex and ever-changing global business environment (Treviño & Nelson, 2014).

In conclusion, the Golden Rule's universal message of empathy and reciprocity provides a robust ethical framework for leadership. By embracing this principle, leaders can transform their leadership style and create a legacy that transcends the bottom line, touching lives and driving meaningful change. Understanding and applying the Golden Rule across cultures and religions enables leaders to build stronger teams, make more ethical decisions, and achieve sustainable success (Johnson, 2022).

References

Gensler, H. J. (2013). *Ethics and the Golden Rule*. Routledge.

Harrison, T. (2019). *Greek ethics and the philosophical foundation of democracy*. Cambridge University Press.

Johnson, L. (2017). *Global ethics and the environment: A leadership approach*. Springer.

Johnson, L. (2022). *Global ethics and the environment: A leadership approach*. Springer.

Kapoor, I. (2020). *Ethics in international development: Bridging the gap between theory and practice*. Bloomsbury Publishing.

Klostermaier, K. (2018). *A survey of Hinduism*. State University of New York Press.

Lee, K. (2018). *Confucianism and modern leadership*. Brill.

Miller, D. (2019). *The ethics of love: An essay on James Baldwin, Christianity, and the ethics of decolonization*. Ethics Press.

Rahimi, S. (2021). *Islamic ethics and the trusteeship paradigm: Taha Abderrahmane's philosophy in comparative perspectives*. Brill.

Solomon, N. (2017). *Judaism: A contemporary philosophical investigation*. Routledge.

Thompson, C. (2020). *Why Buddhism is true: The science and philosophy of meditation and enlightenment*. Simon & Schuster.

Treviño, L. K., & Nelson, K. A. (2014). *Managing business ethics: Straight talk about how to do it right* (6th ed.). Wiley.

Chapter 2

Ethical Leadership Principles

Ethical leadership is the cornerstone of sustainable success in any organization. It goes beyond mere compliance with laws and regulations; it involves leading with integrity, transparency, empathy, and fairness. This chapter delves into the essential components of ethical leadership, exploring how these principles create a foundation for trust, respect, and high performance within organizations. By integrating the Golden Rule into their leadership practices, leaders can cultivate an environment where ethical behavior is the norm and organizational success is a shared goal.

Introduction to Ethical Leadership

Ethical leadership is a style of leadership that is directed by respect for ethical beliefs and values and for the dignity and rights of others. It is about influencing people and creating an environment that encourages ethical behavior and decision-making. Ethical leaders are role models who communicate their values and principles, inspiring their followers to act with integrity and responsibility (Brown & Treviño, 2006).

Leadership involves more than just achieving goals and meeting targets. It also encompasses the way leaders interact with their team members, stakeholders, and the wider community. Ethical leadership emphasizes the importance of these interactions being grounded in respect, fairness, and compassion.

Core Components of Ethical Leadership

The key components of ethical leadership include integrity, transparency, empathy, and fairness. These components are essential for building trust and fostering a positive organizational culture.

Integrity

Integrity is the foundation of ethical leadership. It involves being honest and having strong moral principles. Leaders with integrity are consistent in their actions, values, methods, measures, and principles. They do what is right, even when it is difficult or unpopular (Simons, 2002).

Integrity in leadership means making decisions based on ethical values and principles rather than on personal gain or convenience. It involves being accountable for one's actions and being transparent about decision-making processes. Leaders with integrity inspire trust and confidence in their followers, creating a stable and reliable organizational environment.

Transparency

Transparency involves being open and honest in communications and actions. It means sharing information openly and ensuring that decisions are made in a fair and open manner. Transparent leaders build trust by keeping their team members informed and involved in decision-making processes (Roberts, 2009).

Transparency is crucial for accountability. When leaders are transparent, they provide clear explanations for their decisions and actions, which helps to build trust and credibility. It also encourages a culture of openness and honesty within the organization, where team members feel comfortable sharing their ideas, concerns, and feedback.

Empathy

Empathy is the ability to understand and share the feelings of others. It is a crucial component of ethical leadership, as it allows leaders to connect with their team members on a deeper level. Empathetic leaders are aware of their team members' needs, concerns, and aspirations, and they use this understanding to guide their actions and decisions (Gentry, Weber, & Sadri, 2007).

Empathy in leadership involves active listening, showing genuine concern for others, and being responsive to their needs. It creates a supportive and inclusive work environment where team members feel valued and respected. Empathetic leaders are better equipped to resolve conflicts, build strong relationships, and foster a collaborative and cohesive team culture.

Fairness

Fairness involves treating people equitably and without bias. Ethical leaders ensure that their decisions and actions are just and impartial, and they strive to create a level playing field for all team members. Fairness in leadership means recognizing and rewarding merit, providing equal opportunities, and addressing any forms of discrimination or favoritism (Tyler & Lind, 1992).

Fairness is essential for building trust and respect within the organization. When leaders are fair, they create an environment where team members feel confident that they will be treated justly and that their contributions will be recognized and valued. This fosters a sense of belonging and commitment, which is crucial for team cohesion and high performance.

The Integration of the Golden Rule

The Golden Rule, which advises treating others as you would like to be treated, is a powerful ethical guideline that can enhance the core components of ethical leadership. By integrating the Golden Rule into their leadership practices, leaders can create a culture of mutual respect, trust, and collaboration.

Applying the Golden Rule

Applying the Golden Rule in leadership involves putting oneself in others' shoes and considering their perspectives and needs. This approach aligns with the principles of empathy, fairness, integrity, and transparency, and it helps leaders make decisions that are ethical and considerate of others' well-being (Gensler, 2013).

For example, a leader who practices the Golden Rule would ensure that their team members have the resources and support they need to succeed. They would be transparent in their communications, sharing information openly and honestly. They would listen to their team members' concerns and take their feedback into account when making decisions. They would treat everyone fairly, provide equal opportunities, and recognize and reward merit.

Benefits of Integrating the Golden Rule

Integrating the Golden Rule into leadership practices has several benefits. It fosters a positive organizational culture where ethical behavior is valued and encouraged. It builds trust and respect among team members, which enhances collaboration and teamwork. It improves employee engagement and satisfaction, as team members feel valued and respected. It also enhances organizational performance, as ethical leaders are more likely to make decisions that are in the best interests of the organization and its stakeholders (Johnson, 2022).

Ethical Decision-Making

Ethical decision-making is a critical aspect of ethical leadership. It involves making choices that are consistent with ethical principles and values and that consider the impact on all stakeholders. Ethical leaders use a systematic approach to decision-making, ensuring that their choices are fair, transparent, and considerate of others' well-being.

Steps in Ethical Decision-Making

1. **Identify the Ethical Issue**: The first step in ethical decision-making is to recognize the ethical issue at hand. This involves identifying the potential impact on stakeholders and the ethical principles that are involved.

2. **Gather Information**: Once the ethical issue has been identified, the next step is to gather relevant information. This includes understanding the facts, identifying the stakeholders, and considering the potential consequences of different courses of action (Treviño & Nelson, 2014).

3. **Evaluate Alternatives**: After gathering information, the next step is to evaluate the different alternatives. This involves considering the ethical principles and values that are relevant to the decision and assessing the potential impact on stakeholders.

4. **Make a Decision**: Based on the evaluation of alternatives, the next step is to make a decision. This involves choosing the course of action that is most consistent with ethical principles and values and that best serves the interests of stakeholders.

5. **Implement the Decision**: Once a decision has been made, the next step is to implement it. This involves taking the necessary actions to carry out the decision and communicating it clearly to all stakeholders.

6. Evaluate the Outcome: The final step in ethical decision-making is to evaluate the outcome. This involves assessing the impact of the decision on stakeholders and determining whether it achieved the desired results. It also involves reflecting on the decision-making process and identifying any lessons learned.

Challenges in Ethical Decision-Making

Ethical decision-making can be challenging, as it often involves complex and competing interests. Leaders may face pressure to prioritize short-term gains over long-term ethical considerations or to make decisions that benefit certain stakeholders at the expense of others. Additionally, ethical decision-making requires a high level of self-awareness and moral courage, as leaders must be willing to stand up for their values and principles, even in the face of opposition.

Strategies for Overcoming Challenges

To overcome these challenges, leaders can use several strategies. One approach is to create a culture of ethical behavior within the organization, where ethical decision-making is valued and encouraged. This involves setting clear ethical standards, providing training and support for ethical decision-making, and recognizing and rewarding ethical behavior (Kaptein, 2011).

Another strategy is to seek input from others. By involving team members and stakeholders in the decision-making process, leaders can gain different perspectives and insights, which can help them make more informed and ethical decisions.

Finally, leaders can use ethical decision-making frameworks and tools to guide their choices. These frameworks provide a structured approach to decision-making, helping leaders consider the ethical principles and values that are relevant to their choices and assess the potential impact on stakeholders.

Building an Ethical Organizational Culture

An ethical organizational culture is one where ethical behavior is valued, encouraged, and rewarded. It is a culture where team members feel confident that they will be treated with respect and fairness and where they are encouraged to act with integrity and responsibility.

Creating a Vision and Values Statement

Creating a vision and values statement is an important step in building an ethical organizational culture. This statement outlines the organization's commitment to ethical behavior and sets the tone for how team members are expected to act. It should reflect the organization's core values and principles and provide clear guidance on what is expected of team members (Schein, 2010).

Leading by Example

Leaders play a crucial role in building an ethical organizational culture. They set the tone for the organization by modeling ethical behavior and demonstrating their commitment to ethical principles. When leaders act with integrity, transparency, empathy, and fairness, they inspire their team members to do the same (Grojean, Resick, Dickson, & Smith, 2004).

Providing Training and Support

Providing training and support for ethical behavior is another important aspect of building an ethical organizational culture. This includes providing training on ethical decision-making, communication, and conflict resolution, as well as providing support for team members who face ethical dilemmas.

Recognizing and Rewarding Ethical Behavior

Recognizing and rewarding ethical behavior is a key component of building an ethical organizational culture. This involves acknowledging and celebrating team members who act with integrity and responsibility and providing incentives for ethical behavior. By recognizing and rewarding ethical behavior, leaders reinforce the importance of ethical principles and encourage team members to act in accordance with them (McQuade, 2022).

Encouraging Open Communication

Open communication is essential for building an ethical organizational culture. This involves creating an environment where team members feel comfortable sharing their ideas, concerns, and feedback and where they are encouraged to speak up about ethical issues. Leaders can encourage open communication by being approachable, listening actively, and responding to concerns in a respectful and constructive manner (Argyris, 1990).

Addressing Unethical Behavior

Addressing unethical behavior is another important aspect of building an ethical organizational culture. This involves taking swift and appropriate action when unethical behavior occurs and ensuring that team members are held accountable for their actions. By addressing unethical behavior, leaders send a clear message that ethical behavior is valued and that violations of ethical principles will not be tolerated.

Case Studies and Real-World Examples

To illustrate the principles of ethical leadership, this section presents several case studies and real-world examples of leaders who have successfully integrated ethical principles into their leadership practices.

Case Study 1: Patagonia

Patagonia, an outdoor clothing and gear company, is known for its strong commitment to ethical leadership and environmental sustainability. The company's founder, Yvon Chouinard, has built a culture that values integrity, transparency, empathy, and fairness. Patagonia's commitment to ethical principles is reflected in its decision-making processes, corporate governance, and community engagement.

For example, Patagonia has implemented several initiatives to reduce its environmental impact, such as using sustainable materials, reducing waste, and promoting environmental conservation. The company also practices transparency by openly sharing information about its supply chain and environmental impact. Additionally, Patagonia values empathy and fairness by providing a supportive work environment, offering fair wages and benefits, and involving employees in decision-making processes (Chouinard & Stanley, 2022).

Case Study 2: Starbucks

Starbucks is another example of a company that has integrated ethical principles into its leadership practices. Under the leadership of its former CEO, Howard Schultz, Starbucks has built a culture that values integrity, transparency, empathy, and fairness. Schultz's commitment to ethical leadership is reflected in the company's policies and practices, such as providing fair wages and benefits, promoting diversity and inclusion, and engaging in corporate social responsibility initiatives.

For example, Starbucks has implemented several programs to support its employees, such as offering health benefits, stock options, and education assistance. The company also practices transparency by openly sharing information about its business practices and performance. Additionally, Starbucks values empathy and fairness by promoting a diverse and inclusive work environment and by engaging in community service and environmental sustainability initiatives (Schultz & Yang, 2011).

Case Study 3: The Body Shop

The Body Shop, a global beauty and cosmetics company, is known for its strong commitment to ethical leadership and social responsibility. The company's founder, Anita Roddick, built a culture that values integrity, transparency, empathy, and fairness. The Body Shop's commitment to ethical principles is reflected in its decision-making processes, corporate governance, and community engagement.

For example, The Body Shop has implemented several initiatives to promote social and environmental sustainability, such as using ethically sourced ingredients, reducing waste, and promoting fair trade. The company also practices transparency by openly sharing information about its supply chain and environmental impact. Additionally, The Body Shop values empathy and fairness by providing a supportive work environment, offering fair wages and benefits, and involving employees in decision-making processes (Roddick, 2005).

Conclusion

Ethical leadership is essential for creating a positive organizational culture and achieving sustainable success. By integrating the core components of ethical leadership—integrity, transparency, empathy, and fairness—leaders can build trust, foster collaboration, and inspire high performance within their organizations. The Golden Rule provides a powerful ethical guideline that enhances these principles, helping leaders create a culture of mutual respect, trust, and collaboration.

By applying the Golden Rule and practicing ethical decision-making, leaders can navigate complex and competing interests, make choices that are fair and considerate of others' well-being, and build an ethical organizational culture. The case studies and real-world examples presented in this chapter illustrate the benefits of ethical leadership and provide practical insights for leaders seeking to integrate ethical principles into their leadership practices.

As we move forward in this book, we will continue to explore the profound implications of ethical leadership and the Golden Rule in various leadership contexts. We will delve into how these principles influence leadership behaviors, shape organizational cultures, and optimize operational effectiveness across diverse cultural landscapes. Through this exploration, we aim to provide deeper insights into the role of ethical leadership in fostering sustainable success and positive organizational climates.

References

Argyris, C. (1990). *Overcoming organizational defenses: Facilitating organizational learning*. Allyn & Bacon.

Brown, M. E., & Treviño, L. K. (2006). Ethical leadership: A review and future directions. *The Leadership Quarterly, 17*(6), 595-616.

Chouinard, Y., & Stanley, V. (2023). The future of the responsible company: What we've learned from Patagonia's first 50 Years. Patagonia.

Gentry, W. A., Weber, T. J., & Sadri, G. (2007). Empathy in the workplace: A tool for effective leadership. *Society for Human Resource Management*.

Gensler, H. J. (2013). *Ethics and the Golden Rule*. Routledge.

Grojean, M. W., Resick, C. J., Dickson, M. W., & Smith, D. B. (2004). Leaders, values, and organizational climate: Examining leadership strategies for establishing an organizational climate regarding ethics. *Journal of Business Ethics, 55*(3), 223-241.

Johnson, L. (2022). *Global ethics and the environment: A leadership approach*. Springer.

Kaptein, M. (2011). Understanding unethical behavior by unraveling ethical culture. *Human Relations, 64*(6), 843-869.

McQuade, A. (2022). Ethical leadership: *Moral decision-making under pressure*. Walter deGruyter GmbH.

Roberts, J. (2009). No one is perfect: The limits of transparency and an ethic for 'intelligent' accountability. *Accounting, Organizations and Society, 34*(8), 957-970.

Roddick, A. (2005). *Business as unusual: My entrepreneurial journey, profits with principles*. Anita Roddick Books.

Schein, E. H. (2010). *Organizational culture and leadership* (4th ed.). Jossey-Bass.

Schultz, H., & Yang, D. J. (2011). *Onward: How Starbucks fought for its life without losing its soul*. Rodale Books.

Simons, T. (2002). Behavioral integrity: The perceived alignment between managers' words and deeds as a research focus. *Organization Science, 13*(1), 18-35.

Treviño, L. K., & Nelson, K. A. (2014). *Managing business ethics: Straight talk about how to do it right* (6th ed.). Wiley.

Tyler, T. R., & Lind, E. A. (1992). A relational model of authority in groups. *Advances in Experimental Social Psychology, 25*, 115-191.

Chapter 3

Defining Alignment of Purpose

In today's complex and competitive business environment, the alignment of purpose is a crucial factor for achieving sustainable success. Alignment of purpose refers to the congruence between organizational goals and the personal values and objectives of its members. When leaders align these elements effectively, they create a harmonious work environment that enhances employee engagement, satisfaction, and productivity. This chapter explores the concept of alignment of purpose, its importance, the benefits it offers, and the strategies leaders can use to achieve it within their organizations.

Explanation of Alignment of Purpose

Alignment of purpose is the process of ensuring that the goals of the organization are in harmony with the personal values and objectives of its employees. This alignment is essential for fostering a sense of meaning and fulfillment among team members, which in turn drives organizational performance. When employees feel that their personal values are aligned with the organization's mission and goals, they are more likely to be motivated, committed, and engaged in their work (Cartwright & Holmes, 2006).

At its core, alignment of purpose involves creating a shared vision that resonates with both the organization and its members. This shared vision serves as a guiding light for decision-making, goal-setting, and daily operations. It ensures that everyone in the organization is working towards a common goal, which enhances coherence and collaboration.

Importance of Alignment of Purpose

The importance of alignment of purpose cannot be overstated. Organizations with strong alignment between their goals and the personal values of their employees experience numerous benefits, including increased engagement, higher job satisfaction, improved retention rates, and enhanced organizational performance (Collins & Porras, 1996).

Enhanced Employee Engagement

Employee engagement is a critical factor in organizational success. Engaged employees are more productive, innovative, and committed to their work. When employees' personal values align with the organization's goals, they are more likely to be engaged because they feel that their work is meaningful and contributes to a greater purpose (Peters, 2019). This sense of purpose fosters intrinsic motivation, which drives employees to go above and beyond in their roles.

Higher Job Satisfaction

Job satisfaction is closely linked to the alignment of purpose. When employees feel that their work aligns with their personal values and goals, they are more likely to be satisfied with their jobs. This satisfaction stems from the sense of fulfillment and accomplishment that comes from working towards a meaningful goal (Locke & Latham, 1990). Higher job satisfaction, in turn, leads to better performance and lower turnover rates.

Improved Retention Rates

Retention rates are significantly influenced by the alignment of purpose. Employees who feel that their personal values align with the organization's mission are less likely to leave the organization. This is because they feel a strong connection to the organization and believe that their work is making a difference (Meyer & Allen, 1991). Improved retention rates reduce the costs associated with hiring and training new employees, and they ensure that the organization retains its top talent.

Enhanced Organizational Performance

Organizations with a strong alignment of purpose tend to perform better overall. This is because alignment fosters a sense of unity and collaboration among employees, which enhances efficiency and effectiveness (Collins & Porras, 1996). When everyone in the organization is working towards a common goal, there is less confusion, fewer conflicts, and more synergy. This collaborative environment drives innovation, improves decision-making, and enhances overall organizational performance.

Case Studies Illustrating Effective Alignment of Purpose

Case Study 1: Patagonia

Patagonia, an outdoor clothing and gear company, is renowned for its strong alignment of purpose. The company's mission statement, "We're in business to save our home planet," resonates deeply with its employees, who are passionate about environmental conservation and sustainability (Chouinard & Stanley, 2022). Patagonia aligns its organizational goals with the personal values of its employees by focusing on sustainability, ethical manufacturing practices, and environmental activism.

The company's commitment to these principles is evident in its business practices, such as using recycled materials, reducing waste, and donating a portion of its profits to environmental causes. Patagonia's employees are deeply engaged and motivated because they believe in the company's mission and see their work as contributing to the greater good. This strong alignment of purpose has resulted in high employee satisfaction, low turnover rates, and strong organizational performance.

Case Study 2: Zappos

Zappos, an online shoe and clothing retailer, is another example of a company with a strong alignment of purpose. Zappos' mission is to "deliver happiness to customers, employees, and vendors," and its core values emphasize customer service, innovation, and community (Hsieh, 2010). Zappos aligns its organizational goals with the personal values of its employees by creating a culture that prioritizes customer satisfaction and employee well-being.

The company's commitment to these values is reflected in its business practices, such as providing exceptional customer service, fostering a fun and inclusive work environment, and offering extensive employee benefits and development opportunities. Zappos' employees are highly engaged and motivated because they believe in the company's mission and feel valued and supported in their roles. This strong alignment of purpose has resulted in high employee satisfaction, low turnover rates, and strong organizational performance.

Challenges and Solutions

While the benefits of alignment of purpose are clear, achieving this alignment can be challenging. Organizations often face obstacles such as misalignment between organizational goals and employee values, resistance to change, and difficulties in communication. However, there are several strategies that leaders can use to overcome these challenges and achieve alignment of purpose within their organizations.

Challenge 1: Misalignment Between Organizational Goals and Employee Values

One of the biggest challenges in achieving alignment of purpose is the potential for misalignment between organizational goals and employee values. This misalignment can occur when employees feel that the organization's goals do not align with their personal values and aspirations. To address this challenge, leaders can take the following steps:

1. **Assess and Align Organizational Values**: Leaders should regularly assess the organization's values and ensure that they align with the personal values of their employees. This involves engaging employees in discussions about the organization's mission and goals and making adjustments as needed to ensure alignment.

2. **Communicate the Organization's Mission and Values**: Clear and consistent communication is essential for achieving alignment of purpose. Leaders should regularly communicate the organization's mission and values to employees and ensure that these messages are reinforced through actions and behaviors.

3. **Involve Employees in Goal-Setting**: Involving employees in the goal-setting process can help ensure that organizational goals align with their personal values. Leaders should seek input from employees when setting goals and objectives and ensure that these goals resonate with their values and aspirations.

Challenge 2: Resistance to Change

Resistance to change is another common challenge in achieving alignment of purpose. Employees may resist changes to the organization's mission, values, or goals, particularly if they feel that these changes do not align with their personal values. To address this challenge, leaders can take the following steps:

1. **Engage Employees in the Change Process**: Engaging employees in the change process can help reduce resistance and ensure alignment. Leaders should involve employees in discussions about changes to the organization's mission, values, or goals and seek their input and feedback.

2. **Communicate the Benefits of Change**: Clear and consistent communication about the benefits of change can help reduce resistance and ensure alignment. Leaders should explain why changes are being made, how they align with the organization's mission and values, and how they will benefit employees and the organization as a whole.

3. **Provide Support and Resources**: Providing support and resources can help employees adapt to changes and ensure alignment. Leaders should offer training, development opportunities, and other resources to help employees understand and embrace changes to the organization's mission, values, or goals.

Challenge 3: Difficulties in Communication

Effective communication is essential for achieving alignment of purpose, but it can be challenging to ensure that messages are clear, consistent, and resonate with employees. To address this challenge, leaders can take the following steps:

1. **Develop a Clear Communication Strategy**: Developing a clear communication strategy can help ensure that messages are clear, consistent, and resonate with employees. This involves identifying key messages, determining the best channels for communication, and ensuring that messages are reinforced through actions and behaviors.

2. **Use Multiple Communication Channels**: Using multiple communication channels can help ensure that messages reach all employees and resonate with different communication preferences. Leaders should use a variety of channels, such as emails, meetings, newsletters, and social media, to communicate the organization's mission and values.

3. **Encourage Open and Transparent Communication**: Encouraging open and transparent communication can help ensure alignment of purpose. Leaders should create an environment where

employees feel comfortable sharing their ideas, concerns, and feedback and where they are encouraged to speak up about alignment issues.

Leadership's Role in Achieving Alignment of Purpose

Leadership plays a critical role in achieving alignment of purpose within organizations. Effective leaders create a shared vision, communicate the organization's mission and values, and engage employees in the goal-setting process. They also model ethical behavior, build trust, and create an inclusive and supportive work environment.

Creating a Shared Vision

Creating a shared vision is essential for achieving alignment of purpose. A shared vision serves as a guiding light for decision-making, goal-setting, and daily operations, ensuring that everyone in the organization is working towards a common goal. Leaders can create a shared vision by engaging employees in discussions about the organization's mission and goals and ensuring that these resonate with their values and aspirations (Collins & Porras, 1996).

Communicating the Organization's Mission and Values

Clear and consistent communication is essential for achieving alignment of purpose. Leaders should regularly communicate the organization's mission and values to employees and ensure that these messages are reinforced through actions and behaviors. This involves using multiple communication channels, providing regular updates, and ensuring that messages are clear, consistent, and resonate with employees (Roberts, 2009).

Engaging Employees in the Goal-Setting Process

Involving employees in the goal-setting process can help ensure that organizational goals align with their personal values. Leaders should seek input from employees when setting goals and objectives and ensure that these goals resonate with their values and aspirations. This involves creating opportunities for employees to contribute to goal-setting discussions, providing feedback on goals, and involving employees in decision-making processes (Locke & Latham, 1990).

Modeling Ethical Behavior

Leaders play a critical role in modeling ethical behavior and creating a culture of integrity and trust. By acting with integrity, transparency, empathy, and fairness, leaders set the tone for the organization and inspire employees to do the same. This involves making decisions based on ethical principles, being accountable for actions, and demonstrating a commitment to ethical behavior in all aspects of leadership (Brown & Treviño, 2006).

Building Trust

Building trust is essential for achieving alignment of purpose. Trust fosters collaboration, enhances communication, and creates a supportive and inclusive work environment. Leaders can build trust by being transparent, consistent, and reliable in their actions and communications. This involves keeping promises, being honest, and demonstrating a commitment to the well-being of employees and the organization (Mayer, Davis, & Schoorman, 1995).

Creating an Inclusive and Supportive Work Environment

Creating an inclusive and supportive work environment is essential for achieving alignment of purpose. Leaders should create an environment where employees feel valued, respected, and supported and where they are encouraged to share their ideas, concerns, and feedback. This involves promoting diversity and inclusion, providing opportunities for growth and development, and creating a culture of open and transparent communication (Shore et al., 2011).

Strategies for Achieving Alignment of Purpose

Achieving alignment of purpose requires a strategic and intentional approach. Leaders can use several strategies to ensure that organizational goals align with the personal values and objectives of their employees.

Strategy 1: Develop a Clear Mission and Vision Statement

Developing a clear mission and vision statement is essential for achieving alignment of purpose. These statements should reflect the organization's core values and goals and resonate with the personal values of employees. Leaders should engage employees in the development of these statements, seek their input and feedback, and ensure that the final statements align with their values and aspirations (Collins & Porras, 1996).

Strategy 2: Foster a Culture of Open Communication

Fostering a culture of open communication is essential for achieving alignment of purpose. Leaders should create an environment where employees feel comfortable sharing their ideas, concerns, and feedback and where they are encouraged to speak up about alignment issues. This involves promoting transparency, providing regular updates, and using multiple communication channels to ensure that messages are clear, consistent, and resonate with employees (Roberts, 2009).

Strategy 3: Involve Employees in Goal-Setting and Decision-Making

Involving employees in the goal-setting and decision-making process is essential for achieving alignment of purpose. Leaders should seek input from employees when setting goals and objectives and ensure that these goals resonate with their values and aspirations. This involves creating opportunities for employees to contribute to goal-setting discussions, providing feedback on goals, and involving employees in decision-making processes (Locke & Latham, 1990).

Strategy 4: Provide Opportunities for Growth and Development

Providing opportunities for growth and development is essential for achieving alignment of purpose. Leaders should create opportunities for employees to develop their skills and advance in their careers and ensure that these opportunities align with their personal values and goals. This involves offering training and development programs, providing mentorship and coaching, and creating a culture of continuous learning and development (London, 2014).

Strategy 5: Recognize and Reward Alignment

Recognizing and rewarding alignment is essential for achieving alignment of purpose. Leaders should acknowledge and celebrate employees who demonstrate alignment between their personal values and the organization's goals. This involves providing recognition and rewards for alignment, creating opportunities for employees to share their alignment stories, and promoting a culture of alignment and appreciation (Kouzes & Posner, 2017).

Conclusion

The alignment of purpose is a crucial factor for achieving sustainable success in today's complex and competitive business environment. When leaders align organizational goals with the personal values and objectives of their employees, they create a harmonious work environment that enhances employee engagement, satisfaction, and productivity. By creating a shared vision, communicating the organization's mission and values, engaging employees in the goal-setting process, modeling ethical behavior, building trust, and creating an inclusive and supportive work environment, leaders can achieve alignment of purpose within their organizations.

The benefits of alignment of purpose are clear: increased engagement, higher job satisfaction, improved retention rates, and enhanced organizational performance. By using strategic and intentional approaches to achieve alignment, leaders can create a culture of mutual respect, trust, and collaboration and drive sustainable success for their organizations.

As we move forward in this book, we will continue to explore the profound implications of alignment of purpose and ethical leadership in various leadership contexts. We will delve into how these principles influence leadership behaviors, shape organizational cultures, and optimize operational effectiveness across diverse cultural landscapes. Through this exploration, we aim to provide deeper insights into the role of alignment of purpose in fostering sustainable success and positive organizational climates.

References

Brown, M. E., & Treviño, L. K. (2006). Ethical leadership: A review and future directions. *The Leadership Quarterly, 17*(6), 595-616.

Cartwright, S., & Holmes, N. (2006). The meaning of work: The challenge of regaining employee engagement and reducing cynicism. *Human Resource Management Review, 16*(2), 199-208.

Chouinard, Y., & Stanley, V. (2023). *The future of the responsible company: What we've learned from Patagonia's first 50 Years.* Patagonia.

Collins, J. C., & Porras, J. I. (1996). Building your company's vision. *Harvard Business Review, 74*(5), 65-77.

Hsieh, T. (2010). *Delivering happiness: A path to profits, passion, and purpose*. Business Plus.

Peters, J. (2019). *Employee engagement: Creating high positive energy at work*. Knowledge Resources.

Kouzes, J. M., & Posner, B. Z. (2017). *The leadership challenge: How to make extraordinary things happen in organizations* (6th ed.). Wiley.

Locke, E. A., & Latham, G. P. (1990). *A theory of goal setting and task performance*. Prentice Hall.

London, M. (2014). *Job feedback: Giving, seeking, and using feedback for performance improvement* (2nd ed.). Routledge.

Mayer, R. C., Davis, J. H., & Schoorman, F. D. (1995). An integrative model of organizational trust. *Academy of Management Review, 20*(3), 709-734.

Meyer, J. P., & Allen, N. J. (1991). A three-component conceptualization of organizational commitment. *Human Resource Management Review, 1*(1), 61-89.

Roberts, J. (2009). No one is perfect: The limits of transparency and an ethic for 'intelligent' accountability. *Accounting, Organizations and Society, 34*(8), 957-970.

Shore, L. M., Cleveland, J. N., & Sanchez, D. (2011). Inclusive workplaces: A review and model. *Human Resource Management Review, 21*(4), 314-323.

Chapter 4

Leadership's Role in Aligning Purpose

In the quest for organizational excellence, the alignment of purpose plays a pivotal role. This alignment refers to the harmonization of organizational goals with the personal values and objectives of employees. Effective leaders are central to achieving this alignment, as they create a shared vision, communicate the organization's mission and values, engage employees in goal-setting processes, and model ethical behavior. This chapter explores the crucial role that leadership plays in aligning purpose, highlighting strategies and real-world examples that demonstrate how leaders can foster a culture of unity and collaboration.

Strategies for Leaders to Align Goals

Alignment of purpose is not an automatic process; it requires deliberate and strategic actions from leaders. Effective leaders employ various strategies to ensure that organizational goals resonate with the personal values of their team members. These strategies include creating a shared vision, engaging in transparent communication, involving employees in decision-making, and fostering a culture of continuous learning and development.

Creating a Shared Vision

A shared vision is essential for aligning purpose within an organization. This vision serves as a guiding light, providing direction and motivation for both leaders and employees. Effective leaders articulate a clear and compelling vision that resonates with the personal values of their team members.

Creating a shared vision involves several key steps:

1. **Engage Employees in Vision Development**: Involving employees in the development of the organization's vision ensures that it reflects their values and aspirations. Leaders should facilitate discussions, workshops, and brainstorming sessions to gather input and feedback from employees.

2. **Articulate the Vision Clearly**: The vision should be communicated clearly and concisely, using language that resonates with employees. It should be inspiring and motivating, providing a sense of purpose and direction.

3. **Reinforce the Vision Regularly**: Leaders should consistently reinforce the vision through their actions and communications. This involves integrating the vision into daily operations, decision-making processes, and performance evaluations.

Communication and Vision-Sharing Techniques

Transparent and effective communication is crucial for aligning purpose. Leaders must ensure that their communication strategies are clear, consistent, and resonate with employees. This involves using multiple communication channels, providing regular updates, and creating opportunities for open dialogue.

Clear and Consistent Communication

Leaders should communicate the organization's mission, values, and goals clearly and consistently. This involves developing a communication strategy that outlines key messages, identifies target audiences, and determines the best channels for communication.

Multiple Communication Channels

Using multiple communication channels ensures that messages reach all employees and resonate with different communication preferences. Leaders should use a variety of channels, such as emails, meetings, newsletters, social media, and intranet platforms, to communicate the organization's mission and values.

Regular Updates

Providing regular updates keeps employees informed about the organization's progress toward its goals. Leaders should share updates on key initiatives, achievements, and challenges, highlighting how these align with the organization's mission and values.

Open Dialogue

Encouraging open dialogue fosters a culture of transparency and trust. Leaders should create opportunities for employees to share their ideas, concerns, and feedback. This involves holding town hall meetings, Q&A sessions, and feedback forums where employees feel comfortable speaking up and engaging in meaningful conversations.

Case Study: Salesforce

Salesforce's commitment to transparency and open communication is evident in its leadership practices. The company's leaders regularly hold town hall meetings, where employees can ask questions and share their feedback. Salesforce's intranet platform, Chatter, provides a space for employees to engage in discussions and stay informed about company updates. This transparent communication fosters a sense of trust and alignment, as employees feel connected to the organization's mission and values (Benioff & Adler, 2019).

The Impact of Leadership Behavior on Alignment

Leaders set the tone for the organization through their behavior. Ethical leadership, characterized by integrity, transparency, empathy, and fairness, plays a crucial role in aligning purpose. When leaders model ethical behavior, they inspire trust and respect among employees, fostering a culture of alignment and collaboration.

Integrity

Integrity involves being honest and having strong moral principles. Leaders with integrity are consistent in their actions and decisions, which builds trust and credibility. This trust is essential for aligning purpose, as employees are more likely to follow leaders who demonstrate integrity.

Transparency

Transparency involves being open and honest in communications and actions. Transparent leaders share information openly, which fosters a culture of trust and accountability. This transparency ensures that employees understand the organization's mission and values and how their work contributes to these goals.

Empathy

Empathy is the ability to understand and share the feelings of others. Empathetic leaders connect with their team members on a deeper level, understanding their needs, concerns, and aspirations. This empathy fosters a supportive and inclusive work environment where employees feel valued and respected.

Fairness

Fairness involves treating people equitably and without bias. Ethical leaders ensure that their decisions and actions are just and impartial. This fairness builds trust and respect within the organization, fostering a sense of unity and collaboration.

Case Study: Patagonia

Patagonia's commitment to ethical leadership is reflected in its business practices and corporate culture. The company's leaders demonstrate integrity by adhering to sustainable and ethical manufacturing practices. They practice transparency by openly sharing information about the company's environmental impact. They show empathy by creating a supportive work environment, offering fair wages and benefits, and involving employees in decision-making processes. This ethical leadership fosters a strong alignment of purpose, as employees feel connected to the company's mission and values (Chouinard & Stanley, 2022).

Engaging Employees in Decision-Making

Involving employees in decision-making processes is crucial for aligning purposes. This engagement ensures that employees feel valued and heard and that their personal values are considered in organizational decisions. Leaders can engage employees in decision-making through participative leadership, collaborative goal-setting, and continuous feedback mechanisms.

Participative Leadership

Participative leadership involves including employees in decision-making processes. This approach fosters a sense of ownership and accountability, as employees are more likely to support decisions that they have contributed to.

Collaborative Goal-Setting

Collaborative goal-setting involves working with employees to set organizational goals and objectives. This approach ensures that goals resonate with employees' personal values and aspirations, fostering alignment and motivation.

Continuous Feedback Mechanisms

Continuous feedback mechanisms provide opportunities for employees to share their ideas, concerns, and feedback. Leaders should create channels for regular feedback, such as surveys, suggestion boxes, and one-on-one meetings. This feedback helps leaders understand employees' perspectives and make informed decisions that align with their values.

Case Study: Zappos

Zappos' commitment to employee engagement is evident in its participative leadership practices. The company's leaders involve employees in decision-making processes through regular town hall meetings and feedback sessions. Zappos' collaborative goal-setting approach ensures that organizational goals resonate with employees' values and aspirations. This engagement fosters a strong alignment of purpose, as employees feel valued and connected to the company's mission (Hsieh, 2010).

Fostering a Culture of Continuous Learning and Development

Continuous learning and development are essential for aligning purpose. Leaders should create opportunities for employees to develop their skills and advance in their careers, ensuring that these opportunities align with their personal values and goals. This approach fosters a culture of growth and innovation, driving organizational success.

Providing Training and Development Programs

Training and development programs help employees acquire new skills and knowledge, enhancing their performance and job satisfaction. Leaders should offer a variety of programs, such as workshops, seminars, and online courses, to cater to different learning preferences.

Offering Mentorship and Coaching

Mentorship and coaching provide personalized guidance and support, helping employees achieve their career goals. Leaders should create mentorship programs that pair employees with experienced mentors who can provide valuable insights and advice.

Creating a Culture of Continuous Learning

A culture of continuous learning encourages employees to seek out new opportunities for growth and development. Leaders can foster this culture by promoting a growth mindset, providing access to learning resources, and recognizing and rewarding continuous learning.

Case Study: General Electric (GE)

General Electric's commitment to continuous learning and development is evident in its leadership practices. The company offers a variety of training and development programs, including its renowned Leadership Development Center. GE's mentorship and coaching programs provide personalized guidance and support for employees. This culture of continuous learning fosters a strong alignment of purpose, as employees feel supported in their growth and development (Immelt, 2017).

Building Trust and Inclusion

Building trust and creating an inclusive work environment is essential for aligning purpose. Trust fosters collaboration and communication, while inclusion ensures that all employees feel valued and respected. Leaders play a crucial role in building trust and inclusion through their actions and behaviors.

Building Trust

Trust is the foundation of a successful organization. Leaders build trust by being transparent, consistent, and reliable in their actions and communications. This involves keeping promises, being honest, and demonstrating a commitment to the well-being of employees and the organization.

Creating an Inclusive Work Environment

Inclusion involves creating a work environment where all employees feel valued, respected, and supported. Leaders can foster inclusion by promoting diversity, providing equal opportunities, and creating a culture of open and transparent communication.

Case Study: Microsoft

Microsoft's commitment to trust and inclusion is evident in its leadership practices. The company's leaders build trust by being transparent in their communications and consistent in their actions. Microsoft's inclusion initiatives, such as its diversity and inclusion programs, ensure that all employees feel valued and respected. This commitment to trust and inclusion fosters a strong alignment of purpose, as employees feel connected to the company's mission and values (Nadella, 2017).

Real-World Applications and Benefits

Research in diverse organizational settings has demonstrated that leaders who align purpose see marked improvements in employee engagement, satisfaction, and organizational performance. The following case studies illustrate the real-world applications and benefits of leadership's role in aligning purpose.

Case Study: Southwest Airlines

Southwest Airlines' commitment to aligning purpose is evident in its leadership practices. The company's leaders create a shared vision that resonates with employees' values, emphasizing customer service, employee satisfaction, and community involvement. Southwest's transparent communication, participative leadership, and focus on continuous learning and development foster a strong alignment of purpose. This alignment has resulted in high employee engagement, low turnover rates, and strong organizational performance (Kelleher, 1997).

Case Study: Unilever

Unilever's commitment to aligning purpose is reflected in its Sustainable Living Plan, which aims to create a positive social and environmental impact while driving business growth. The company's leaders engage employees in the development and implementation of the plan, ensuring that it resonates with their values and aspirations. Unilever's transparent communication, participative leadership, and focus on continuous learning and development foster a strong alignment of purpose. This alignment has resulted in high employee engagement, improved retention rates, and enhanced organizational performance (Polman, 2016).

Case Study: IBM

IBM's commitment to aligning purpose is evident in its leadership practices and corporate culture. The company's leaders create a shared vision that emphasizes innovation, customer service, and social responsibility. IBM's transparent communication, participative leadership, and focus on continuous learning and development foster a strong alignment of purpose. This alignment has resulted in high employee engagement, improved retention rates, and enhanced organizational performance (Rometty, 2019).

Conclusion

Leadership plays a critical role in aligning purpose within organizations. Effective leaders create a shared vision, communicate the organization's mission and values, engage employees in decision-making, and model ethical behavior. They build trust and create an inclusive work environment, fostering a culture of unity and collaboration. By employing strategic and intentional approaches, leaders can ensure that organizational goals resonate with the personal values and objectives of their employees, driving sustainable success.

The benefits of aligning purpose are clear: increased engagement, higher job satisfaction, improved retention rates, and enhanced organizational performance. Through the strategies and real-world examples presented in this chapter, leaders can gain valuable insights into how to foster alignment of purpose within their organizations. As we move forward in this book, we will continue to explore the profound implications of alignment of purpose and ethical leadership in various leadership contexts, providing deeper insights into how these principles influence leadership behaviors, shape organizational cultures, and optimize operational effectiveness across diverse cultural landscapes.

References

Benioff, M., & Adler, C. (2019). *Trailblazer: The power of business as the greatest platform for change*. Currency.

Chouinard, Y., & Stanley, V. (2023). The future of the responsible company: What we've learned from Patagonia's first 50 Years. Patagonia.

Hsieh, T. (2010). *Delivering happiness: A path to profits, passion, and purpose*. Business Plus.

Immelt, J. R. (2017). *Hot seat: What I learned leading a great American company*. Simon & Schuster.

Kelleher, H. W. (1997). *Nuts! Southwest Airlines' crazy recipe for business and personal success*. Bard Press.

Nadella, S. (2017). *Hit refresh: The quest to rediscover Microsoft's soul and imagine a better future for everyone*. Harper Business.

Polman, P. (2016). *Unilever sustainable living plan: Transforming business for the future*. Unilever.

Rometty, G. (2019). *Good power: Leading positive change in our lives, work, and world*. Harvard Business Review Press.

Schmidt, E., & Rosenberg, J. (2014). *How Google works*. Grand Central Publishing.

Chapter 5

Building a Respectful Organizational Culture

A respectful organizational culture is foundational for creating an environment where employees feel valued, trusted, and empowered. Such a culture fosters mutual respect, collaboration, and ethical behavior, driving both individual and organizational success. This chapter explores the strategies for building a respectful organizational culture, the benefits it offers, and the practical applications of the Golden Rule and addresses the recent pushback on Diversity, Equity, and Inclusion (DEI) initiatives, emphasizing that issues arise when DEI overshadows or replaces merit.

Creating a Culture of Mutual Respect

Mutual respect in the workplace involves recognizing and appreciating the inherent value and contributions of each individual. It is the cornerstone of a positive organizational culture, leading to higher levels of employee engagement, satisfaction, and productivity.

Understanding Mutual Respect

Mutual respect is the recognition that every individual has unique strengths, perspectives, and contributions. It involves treating others with dignity, valuing their input, and acknowledging their achievements. This respect extends to all interactions within the organization, from top management to frontline employees.

Benefits of Mutual Respect

1. Enhanced Employee Engagement: When employees feel respected, they are more likely to be engaged and committed to their work. Engaged employees are more productive, innovative, and willing to go the extra mile (Peters, 2019).

2. Improved Collaboration: A culture of respect fosters open communication and collaboration. Employees feel comfortable sharing their ideas and working together to achieve common goals (Edmondson, 1999).

3. Higher Job Satisfaction: Employees who feel respected are more likely to be satisfied with their jobs. This satisfaction leads to lower turnover rates and higher retention (Spector, 2022).

4. Reduced Conflict: Respectful interactions reduce the likelihood of conflicts and misunderstandings. When conflicts do arise, they are more likely to be resolved amicably and constructively (Gelfand, Leslie, Keller, & de Dreu, 2012).

Strategies for Fostering Mutual Respect

Building a culture of mutual respect requires intentional efforts from leaders and employees alike. The following strategies can help foster respect within the organization:

1. Promote Open Communication

Open communication is essential for building mutual respect. Leaders should create an environment where employees feel comfortable sharing their ideas, concerns, and feedback.

- **Encourage Open Dialogue**: Hold regular meetings and forums where employees can voice their opinions and ask questions. Ensure that these discussions are respectful and inclusive.

- **Listen Actively**: Practice active listening by giving employees your full attention, acknowledging their input, and responding thoughtfully. This demonstrates that you value their contributions.

- **Provide Constructive Feedback**: Offer feedback that is specific, constructive, and aimed at helping employees improve. Avoid criticism that is personal or demotivating.

Case Study: Google

Google's open communication culture is a key factor in its success. The company encourages open dialogue through regular town hall meetings, Q&A sessions with executives, and internal communication platforms. This transparency fosters mutual respect and trust among employees (Schmidt & Rosenberg, 2014).

2. Recognize and Reward Contributions

Recognition and rewards are powerful motivators that reinforce mutual respect. Acknowledging employees' efforts and achievements shows that you value their contributions.

- **Implement Recognition Programs**: Develop programs that recognize and reward employees for their hard work and accomplishments. This can include employee of the month awards, peer recognition, and performance bonuses.

- **Celebrate Milestones**: Celebrate individual and team milestones, such as work anniversaries, project completions, and personal achievements. Public recognition reinforces a sense of belonging and appreciation.

- **Provide Regular Feedback**: Offer regular, positive feedback to employees. Highlight their strengths and contributions, and show appreciation for their efforts.

Case Study: Zappos

Zappos is known for its strong culture of recognition and appreciation. The company has various recognition programs, such as the "Hero Award," which allows employees to nominate their peers for outstanding contributions. This culture of recognition fosters mutual respect and a positive work environment (Hsieh, 2010).

3. Foster Inclusivity and Diversity

Inclusivity and diversity are essential for mutual respect. An inclusive workplace values and respects differences, creating an environment where everyone feels welcome and valued.

- **Promote Diversity and Inclusion**: Implement policies and practices that promote diversity and inclusion. This includes hiring practices, diversity training, and creating employee resource groups.

- **Provide Equal Opportunities**: Ensure that all employees have equal access to opportunities for growth and development. This includes promotions, training programs, and leadership positions.

- **Respect Individual Differences**: Recognize and respect the unique perspectives and experiences of each employee. Encourage a culture of curiosity and openness to different viewpoints.

Case Study: Microsoft

Microsoft's commitment to diversity and inclusion is evident in its leadership practices and corporate policies. The company promotes diversity through initiatives such as the Global Diversity and Inclusion program and employee resource groups. This commitment fosters mutual respect and a supportive work environment (Nadella, 2017).

4. Lead by Example

Leaders play a crucial role in setting the tone for mutual respect within the organization. By modeling respectful behavior, leaders can inspire their employees to do the same.

- **Demonstrate Respectful Behavior**: Treat all employees with dignity and respect. Show appreciation for their contributions and acknowledge their achievements.

- **Be Transparent and Honest**: Communicate openly and honestly with employees. Be transparent about organizational goals, challenges, and decisions.

- **Encourage Ethical Behavior**: Promote ethical behavior by adhering to the organization's values and principles. Address any unethical behavior promptly and appropriately.

Case Study: Patagonia

Patagonia's leaders demonstrate a strong commitment to ethical behavior and respect for employees. The company's leadership practices, such as transparent communication and ethical decision-making, foster a culture of mutual respect and trust (Chouinard & Stanley, 2022).

5. Implement Ethical Guidelines

Ethical guidelines provide a framework for respectful behavior within the organization. By establishing clear expectations and standards, leaders can create a culture of mutual respect.

Develop a Code of Conduct: Create a code of conduct that outlines the organization's values, principles, and expectations for behavior. Ensure that all employees understand and adhere to these guidelines.

- **Provide Ethics Training**: Offer training programs that educate employees on ethical behavior and decision-making. This training should emphasize the importance of respect and integrity in the workplace.

- **Enforce Ethical Standards**: Hold employees accountable for their behavior. Address any violations of the code of conduct promptly and fairly.

Case Study: Johnson & Johnson

Johnson & Johnson's "Credo" serves as the company's ethical framework, outlining its commitment to respect, integrity, and responsibility. The Credo guides the company's decisions and actions, fostering a culture of mutual respect and ethical behavior (Brenner, 2009).

Addressing Pushback on DEI Initiatives

Diversity, Equity, and Inclusion (DEI) initiatives are essential for creating a respectful and inclusive workplace. However, there has been recent pushback against DEI efforts, particularly when they are perceived to overshadow or replace merit-based practices. It is important to address these concerns by emphasizing that DEI and merit are not mutually exclusive but can be integrated effectively.

Understanding DEI Pushback

Pushback against DEI initiatives often stems from the perception that these efforts prioritize diversity over qualifications and performance. Critics argue that this approach can lead to reverse discrimination, where individuals are selected based on their demographic characteristics rather than their skills and abilities.

Balancing DEI and Merit

The key to addressing pushback on DEI initiatives is to ensure that diversity and merit are balanced and integrated effectively. This involves creating policies and practices that promote diversity while also emphasizing the importance of qualifications and performance.

Strategies for Balancing DEI and Merit

1. Transparent Hiring Practices: Develop transparent hiring practices that emphasize both diversity and merit. Ensure that job descriptions and criteria are clear and that the selection process is fair and objective.

2. Diverse Candidate Pools: Proactively seek out diverse candidate pools to ensure a wide range of perspectives and experiences. Use inclusive language in job postings and reach out to diverse networks and communities.

3. Merit-Based Evaluations: Implement merit-based evaluations that focus on qualifications, skills, and performance. Use objective criteria and standardized assessments to evaluate candidates and employees.

4. Inclusive Leadership Development: Provide leadership development opportunities that are accessible to all employees. Encourage diverse candidates to participate in training and mentorship programs to prepare them for leadership roles.

Case Study: IBM

IBM has successfully balanced DEI and merit through its inclusive hiring practices and leadership development programs. The company emphasizes both diversity and performance in its selection processes and provides equal opportunities for growth and development. This approach has helped IBM create a diverse and talented workforce while maintaining high standards of excellence (Rometty, 2019).

The Role of the Golden Rule in DEI

The Golden Rule, which advises treating others as you would like to be treated, is a powerful ethical guideline for balancing DEI and merit. By applying the Golden Rule, leaders can create a culture of respect and fairness that values both diversity and performance.

Applying the Golden Rule to DEI

1. Respect Individual Contributions: Recognize and value the unique contributions of each employee. Treat all employees with dignity and respect, regardless of their background or characteristics.

2. Promote Fairness and Equity: Ensure that all employees have equal access to opportunities and resources. Implement fair and transparent policies that promote equity and inclusion.

3. Foster Open Dialogue: Encourage open and respectful dialogue about diversity and inclusion. Listen to employees' concerns and feedback and address any issues promptly and constructively.

4. Celebrate Diversity: Celebrate the diverse backgrounds and perspectives of employees. Highlight cultural celebrations, awareness days, and other diversity initiatives to promote a sense of belonging and inclusion.

Case Study: Salesforce

Salesforce has successfully applied the Golden Rule to its DEI efforts. The company promotes a culture of respect and fairness by recognizing individual contributions, promoting equity, fostering open dialogue, and celebrating diversity. This approach has helped Salesforce create an inclusive and supportive work environment that values both diversity and performance (Benioff & Adler, 2019).

Building and Sustaining a Respectful Organizational Culture

Building a respectful organizational culture is an ongoing process that requires continuous effort and commitment from leaders and employees alike. The following strategies can help sustain a culture of mutual respect within the organization:

1. Continuous Improvement

Continuous improvement involves regularly assessing and enhancing the organization's culture and practices. Leaders should seek feedback from employees, identify areas for improvement, and implement changes that promote mutual respect.

- **Conduct Regular Surveys**: Use employee surveys to gather feedback on the organization's culture and identify areas for improvement. Ensure that surveys are anonymous to encourage honest responses.

- **Hold Focus Groups**: Organize focus groups to discuss specific issues and gather in-depth feedback from employees. Use this feedback to inform decisions and improvements.

- **Implement Action Plans**: Develop and implement action plans based on feedback and assessments. Monitor progress and make adjustments as needed to ensure continuous improvement.

Case Study: General Electric (GE)

General Electric's commitment to continuous improvement is evident in its leadership practices. The company regularly conducts employee surveys and focus groups to gather feedback on its culture and practices. This commitment to continuous improvement fosters a culture of mutual respect and drives organizational success (Immelt, 2017).

2. Training and Development

Ongoing training and development are essential for sustaining a respectful organizational culture. Leaders should provide regular training programs that reinforce the organization's values and principles.

- **Offer Ethics Training**: Provide regular ethics training that emphasizes the importance of respect, integrity, and ethical behavior. Use real-world scenarios and case studies to illustrate key concepts.

- **Provide Diversity and Inclusion Training**: Offer training programs that promote diversity and inclusion. This training should highlight the benefits of a diverse and inclusive workplace and provide strategies for fostering mutual respect.

- **Encourage Professional Development**: Support employees' professional development by offering training programs, workshops, and seminars. Encourage employees to pursue opportunities for growth and advancement.

Case Study: IBM

IBM's commitment to training and development is evident in its leadership practices and corporate policies. The company offers a variety of training programs, including ethics training and diversity and inclusion training. This commitment to training and development fosters a culture of mutual respect and supports employees' growth and development (Rometty, 2019).

3. Leadership Accountability

Leaders play a crucial role in sustaining a respectful organizational culture. By holding themselves and others accountable for their behavior, leaders can reinforce the organization's values and principles.

- **Set Clear Expectations**: Clearly communicate the organization's values and expectations for behavior. Ensure that all employees understand and adhere to these standards.

- **Lead by Example**: Model respectful behavior in all interactions. Demonstrate a commitment to the organization's values and principles through your actions and decisions.

- **Hold Employees Accountable**: Address any violations of the organization's values and standards promptly and fairly. Ensure that all employees are held accountable for their behavior.

Case Study: Johnson & Johnson

Johnson & Johnson's leaders demonstrate a strong commitment to accountability and ethical behavior. The company's "Credo" outlines its values and expectations for behavior, and leaders are held accountable for adhering to these standards. This commitment to accountability fosters a culture of mutual respect and ethical behavior (Brenner, 2009).

4. Celebrating Diversity and Inclusion

Celebrating diversity and inclusion is essential for sustaining a respectful organizational culture. Leaders should create opportunities to recognize and celebrate the unique perspectives and contributions of all employees.

- **Host Diversity Events**: Organize events that celebrate the diversity of the organization's workforce. This can include cultural celebrations, diversity fairs, and guest speaker events.

- **Recognize Inclusive Practices**: Highlight and reward employees who demonstrate inclusive behavior. Create awards and recognition programs that celebrate diversity and inclusion.

- **Promote Diverse Perspectives**: Encourage employees to share their unique perspectives and experiences. Create platforms for employees to share their stories and insights.

Case Study: Microsoft

Microsoft's commitment to celebrating diversity and inclusion is evident in its leadership practices and corporate policies. The company hosts a variety of diversity events, such as cultural celebrations and guest speaker events, and recognizes employees who demonstrate inclusive behavior. This commitment to celebrating diversity and inclusion fosters a culture of mutual respect and supports a diverse and inclusive workplace (Nadella, 2017).

Conclusion

Building a respectful organizational culture is essential for creating an environment where employees feel valued, trusted, and empowered. By promoting open communication, recognizing and rewarding contributions, fostering inclusivity and diversity, leading by example, and implementing ethical guidelines, leaders can create a culture of mutual respect and collaboration.

The Golden Rule, which advises treating others as you would like to be treated, provides a powerful ethical guideline for fostering respect within the workplace. By applying the Golden Rule, leaders can create a positive organizational culture where ethical behavior is valued and encouraged.

Addressing pushback on DEI initiatives involves balancing diversity and merit, ensuring that all employees have equal access to opportunities and resources while maintaining high standards of performance. By integrating DEI and merit effectively, leaders can create an inclusive and high-performing work environment.

Sustaining a respectful organizational culture requires continuous effort and commitment from leaders and employees alike. By focusing on continuous improvement, providing ongoing training and development, holding leaders accountable, and celebrating diversity and inclusion, organizations can foster a culture of mutual respect and drive sustainable success.

As we move forward in this book, we will continue to explore the profound implications of ethical leadership and the Golden Rule in various leadership contexts. We will delve into how these principles influence leadership behaviors, shape organizational cultures, and optimize operational effectiveness across diverse cultural landscapes. Through this exploration, we aim to provide deeper insights into the role of ethical leadership in fostering sustainable success and positive organizational climates.

References

Brenner, S. N. (2009). Johnson & Johnson's Credo: A corporate cultural relic or a practical guide to employees. *Journal of Business Ethics, 85*(3), 219-223.

Chouinard, Y., & Stanley, V. (2023). *The future of the responsible company: What we've learned from Patagonia's first 50 Years*. Patagonia.

Edmondson, A. (1999). Psychological safety and learning behavior in work teams. *Administrative Science Quarterly, 44*(2), 350-383.

Gelfand, M. J., Leslie, L. M., Keller, K. M., & de Dreu, C. K. (2012). Conflict cultures in organizations: How leaders shape conflict cultures and their organizational-level consequences. *Journal of Applied Psychology, 97*(6), 1131-1147.

Gensler, H. J. (2013). *Ethics and the Golden Rule*. Routledge.

Hsieh, T. (2010). *Delivering happiness: A path to profits, passion, and purpose*. Business Plus.

Immelt, J. R. (2017). *Hot seat: What I learned leading a great American company*. Simon & Schuster.

Johnson, L. (2022). *Global ethics and the environment: A leadership approach*. Springer.

Peters, J. (2019). *Employee engagement: Creating high positive energy at work*. Knowledge Resources.

Spector, P. E. (2022). *Job satisfaction: From assessment to intervention*. Routledge.

Nadella, S. (2017). *Hit refresh: The quest to rediscover Microsoft's soul and imagine a better future for everyone*. Harper Business.

Roddick, A. (2005). *Business as unusual: My entrepreneurial journey, profits with principles*. Anita Roddick Books.

Rometty, G. (2019). *Good power: Leading positive change in our lives, work, and world*. Harvard Business Review Press.

Schmidt, E., & Rosenberg, J. (2014). *How Google works*. Grand Central Publishing.

Chapter 6

Enhancing Employee Engagement and Productivity

Employee engagement and productivity are critical drivers of organizational success. Engaged employees are more committed, motivated, and productive, contributing to a positive work environment and better overall performance. This chapter explores the importance of the Golden Rule in enhancing employee engagement and productivity, providing practical strategies and real-world examples of how ethical leadership can foster a supportive and motivating work environment.

The Role of the Golden Rule in Employee Engagement

The Golden Rule, which advises treating others as you would like to be treated, is a powerful ethical guideline for enhancing employee engagement. By applying the Golden Rule, leaders can create a work environment where employees feel valued, respected, and supported.

Understanding Employee Engagement

Employee engagement is the emotional commitment an employee has toward their organization and its goals. Engaged employees are passionate about their work, willing to go the extra mile, and motivated to contribute to the organization's success (Peters, 2019). Engagement is driven by various factors, including job satisfaction, a sense of purpose, recognition, and a supportive work environment.

Benefits of Employee Engagement

1. **Increased Productivity**: Engaged employees are more productive and efficient in their work. They are motivated to perform at their best

and contribute to the organization's goals (Harter, Schmidt, & Hayes, 2002).

2. Higher Retention Rates: Organizations with high employee engagement experience lower turnover rates. Engaged employees are more likely to stay with the organization, reducing the costs associated with hiring and training new employees (Macey & Schneider, 2008).

3. Improved Customer Satisfaction: Engaged employees are more likely to provide excellent customer service, leading to higher customer satisfaction and loyalty (Saks, 2006).

4. Enhanced Innovation: Engaged employees are more creative and willing to share their ideas. This fosters a culture of innovation where new ideas and solutions are encouraged (Bakker & Demerouti, 2008).

Applying the Golden Rule to Enhance Engagement

The Golden Rule can be applied in various ways to enhance employee engagement:

1. Show Respect and Appreciation: Treat employees with respect and show appreciation for their contributions. This fosters a sense of value and recognition, which drives engagement.

2. Provide Support and Resources: Ensure that employees have the necessary resources and support to perform their jobs effectively. This includes providing training, tools, and a supportive work environment.

3. Communicate Openly and Transparently: Maintain open and transparent communication with employees. Keep them informed about organizational goals, changes, and developments. Encourage feedback and active participation.

4. Offer Opportunities for Growth and Development: Provide opportunities for employees to grow and develop their skills. This includes offering training programs, career development opportunities, and mentorship.

Case Study: Google

Google is renowned for its high levels of employee engagement. The company's leaders apply the Golden Rule by fostering a culture of respect, support, and open communication. Google provides extensive resources and support for employees, including state-of-the-art facilities, continuous learning opportunities, and a collaborative work environment. This commitment to treating employees well has resulted in high engagement, low turnover rates, and strong organizational performance (Schmidt & Rosenberg, 2014).

Creating a Supportive Work Environment

A supportive work environment is essential for enhancing employee engagement and productivity. Leaders play a crucial role in creating such an environment by fostering trust, collaboration, and a sense of belonging.

Building Trust

Trust is the foundation of a supportive work environment. When employees trust their leaders and colleagues, they feel safe to express their ideas, take risks, and collaborate effectively.

Strategies for Building Trust

1. **Demonstrate Integrity**: Act with honesty and integrity in all interactions. Keep promises and be consistent in your actions and decisions.

2. **Communicate Transparently**: Be open and transparent in your communication. Share information honestly and keep employees informed about organizational developments.

3. **Show Empathy**: Understand and appreciate employees' perspectives and needs. Show genuine concern for their well-being and provide support when needed.

4. **Encourage Accountability**: Hold yourself and others accountable for their actions. Address issues promptly and fairly and ensure that everyone adheres to the organization's values and standards.

Case Study: Microsoft

Under the leadership of Satya Nadella, Microsoft has focused on building a culture of trust and empathy. Nadella emphasizes the importance of integrity, transparent communication, and empathy in leadership. This approach has fostered a supportive work environment, leading to higher employee engagement and productivity (Nadella, 2017).

Fostering Collaboration

Collaboration is essential for achieving organizational goals and driving innovation. A collaborative work environment encourages teamwork, knowledge sharing, and collective problem-solving.

Strategies for Fostering Collaboration

1. Encourage Teamwork: Promote teamwork by creating opportunities for employees to work together on projects and initiatives. Provide tools and resources that facilitate collaboration.

2. Create Collaborative Spaces: Design the workplace to include collaborative spaces where employees can gather, brainstorm, and work together. This includes meeting rooms, breakout areas, and open office layouts.

3. Recognize Collaborative Efforts: Recognize and reward employees who demonstrate strong collaboration skills. Highlight successful team projects and celebrate collective achievements.

4. Provide Training on Collaboration: Offer training programs that focus on developing collaboration skills, such as communication, conflict resolution, and teamwork.

Case Study: Zappos

Zappos fosters a culture of collaboration through its unique organizational structure and work environment. The company encourages employees to work together on projects and initiatives, providing collaborative spaces and tools that facilitate teamwork. Zappos' commitment to collaboration has resulted in high employee engagement and innovative solutions (Hsieh, 2010).

Creating a Sense of Belonging

A sense of belonging is essential for employee engagement and productivity. When employees feel that they are part of a supportive and inclusive community, they are more motivated and committed to their work.

Strategies for Creating a Sense of Belonging

1.   **Promote Inclusivity**: Foster an inclusive work environment where all employees feel valued and respected. Implement policies and practices that promote diversity and inclusion.

2. **Encourage Social Connections**: Create opportunities for employees to connect and build relationships. This includes team-building activities, social events, and employee resource groups.

3. **Celebrate Diversity**: Recognize and celebrate the diverse backgrounds and perspectives of employees. Highlight cultural celebrations, awareness days, and other diversity initiatives.

4. **Support Work-Life Balance**: Encourage work-life balance by offering flexible work arrangements, wellness programs, and support for employees' personal and family needs.

Case Study: Salesforce

Salesforce is known for its strong commitment to diversity and inclusion. The company promotes inclusivity through its various initiatives, such as employee resource groups, diversity training programs, and cultural celebrations. Salesforce's focus on creating a sense of belonging has led to high employee engagement and productivity (Benioff & Adler, 2019).

Recognizing and Rewarding Employees

Recognition and rewards are powerful motivators that enhance employee engagement and productivity. By acknowledging employees' efforts and achievements, leaders can reinforce positive behavior and foster a culture of appreciation.

The Importance of Recognition

Recognition is the acknowledgment and appreciation of employees' contributions and achievements. It is a fundamental human need and a critical driver of engagement and motivation (Locke & Latham, 2002).

Benefits of Recognition

1.   **Increased Motivation**: Recognition boosts employees' motivation to perform at their best. It reinforces positive behavior and encourages continued effort.

2. Higher Job Satisfaction: Employees who feel recognized and appreciated are more likely to be satisfied with their jobs. This satisfaction leads to higher engagement and retention (Deci & Ryan, 2000).

3. Enhanced Performance: Recognized employees are more productive and committed to their work. They are willing to go the extra mile to achieve organizational goals (Harter et al., 2002).

Effective Recognition Strategies

1. Provide Timely Recognition: Offer recognition promptly after an achievement or contribution. Timely recognition reinforces the connection between behavior and reward.

2. Use Multiple Recognition Methods: Utilize various methods to recognize employees, such as verbal praise, written notes, awards, and public acknowledgment. This ensures that recognition is meaningful and impactful.

3. Personalize Recognition: Tailor recognition to individual preferences and achievements. Understand what motivates each employee and recognize them in ways that resonate with them.

4. Encourage Peer Recognition: Promote a culture of peer recognition where employees recognize and appreciate each other's contributions. This fosters a sense of community and mutual support.

Case Study: The Body Shop

The Body Shop has implemented various recognition programs to acknowledge employees' contributions and achievements. These programs include the "Values Award," which recognizes employees who exemplify the company's values, and the "Bravo Award," which allows peers to nominate each other for outstanding efforts. The Body Shop's commitment to recognition has resulted in high employee engagement and a positive work environment (Roddick, 2005).

Providing Opportunities for Growth and Development

Opportunities for growth and development are essential for enhancing employee engagement and productivity. When employees see a clear path for career advancement and skill development, they are more motivated and committed to their work.

The Role of Development in Engagement

Professional development involves providing employees with opportunities to acquire new skills, knowledge, and experiences that enhance their performance and career prospects. Development is a key driver of engagement and motivation (London & Smither, 1999).

Benefits of Providing Development Opportunities

1. Increased Employee Retention: Employees who have opportunities for growth are more likely to stay with the organization. Development opportunities signal that the organization values and invests in its employees (Allen, Shore, & Griffeth, 2003).

2. Enhanced Performance: Development opportunities improve employees' skills and capabilities, leading to better performance and productivity. Employees are better equipped to meet the demands of their roles (Aguinis & Kraiger, 2009).

3. Greater Job Satisfaction: Employees who see opportunities for growth are more satisfied with their jobs. This satisfaction leads to higher engagement and motivation (Noe, 2017).

Effective Development Strategies

1. Offer Training Programs: Provide training programs that focus on developing employees' skills and knowledge. This includes workshops, seminars, online courses, and certifications.

2. Provide Mentorship and Coaching: Implement mentorship and coaching programs that offer personalized guidance and support. Pair employees with experienced mentors who can provide valuable insights and advice.

3. Create Career Development Plans: Develop individual career development plans that outline employees' career goals and the steps needed to achieve them. Regularly review and update these plans to ensure progress.

4. Encourage Continuous Learning: Promote a culture of continuous learning where employees are encouraged to seek out new opportunities for growth. Provide access to learning resources, such as libraries, e-learning platforms, and professional development funds.

Case Study: General Electric (GE)

General Electric's commitment to employee development is evident in its leadership practices and corporate policies. The company offers a variety of training programs, including its renowned Leadership Development Center. GE's mentorship and coaching programs provide personalized guidance and support for employees. This focus on development fosters a strong alignment of purpose, as employees feel supported in their growth and development (Immelt, 2017).

Promoting Work-Life Balance

Work-life balance is essential for employee engagement and productivity. When employees can balance their work and personal lives, they are more satisfied and motivated in their roles.

The Importance of Work-Life Balance

Work-life balance involves managing work responsibilities while maintaining a fulfilling personal life. It is crucial for overall well-being and job satisfaction (Greenhaus & Beutell, 1985).

Benefits of Work-Life Balance

1. Reduced Stress: Work-life balance reduces stress and burnout, leading to better mental and physical health. Employees are more focused and productive when they are not overwhelmed by work demands (Kossek & Ozeki, 1998).

2. Higher Job Satisfaction: Employees who can balance their work and personal lives are more satisfied with their jobs. This satisfaction leads to higher engagement and retention (Carlson, Grzywacz, & Zivnuska, 2009).

3. Improved Performance: Employees with a healthy work-life balance are more motivated and productive. They are better able to concentrate and perform their tasks effectively (Allen et al., 2000).

Strategies for Promoting Work-Life Balance

1. Offer Flexible Work Arrangements: Provide flexible work arrangements, such as telecommuting, flexible hours, and compressed workweeks. This allows employees to manage their work and personal responsibilities more effectively.

2. Encourage Time Off: Promote the use of vacation days and encourage employees to take regular breaks. Ensure that employees feel supported when taking time off to recharge.

3. Provide Wellness Programs: Implement wellness programs that support employees' physical and mental health. This includes fitness classes, stress management workshops, and employee assistance programs.

4. Support Family-Friendly Policies: Offer family-friendly policies, such as parental leave, childcare support, and family medical leave. These policies help employees balance their work and family responsibilities.

Case Study: Microsoft

Microsoft's commitment to work-life balance is evident in its leadership practices and corporate policies. The company offers flexible work arrangements, generous parental leave, and comprehensive wellness programs. Microsoft's focus on work-life balance fosters a supportive work environment, leading to higher employee engagement and productivity (Nadella, 2017).

Conclusion

Enhancing employee engagement and productivity is essential for organizational success. By applying the Golden Rule and fostering a supportive work environment, leaders can create a culture where employees feel valued, respected, and motivated. Strategies such as building trust, fostering collaboration, creating a sense of belonging, recognizing and rewarding employees, providing development opportunities, and promoting work-life balance are critical for achieving high levels of engagement and productivity.

The benefits of enhanced employee engagement and productivity are clear: increased motivation, higher job satisfaction, improved retention rates, and better overall performance. Through the strategies and real-world examples presented in this chapter, leaders can gain valuable insights into how to foster a supportive and engaging work environment. As we move forward in this book, we will continue to explore the profound implications of ethical leadership and the Golden Rule in various leadership contexts, providing deeper insights into how these principles influence leadership behaviors, shape organizational cultures, and optimize operational effectiveness across diverse cultural landscapes.

References

Aguinis, H., & Kraiger, K. (2009). Benefits of training and development for individuals and teams, organizations, and society. *Annual Review of Psychology, 60*, 451-474.

Allen, D. G., Shore, L. M., & Griffeth, R. W. (2003). The role of perceived organizational support and supportive human resource practices in the turnover process. *Journal of Management, 29*(1), 99-118.

Allen, T. D., Herst, D. E. L., Bruck, C. S., & Sutton, M. (2000). Consequences associated with work-to-family conflict: A review and agenda for future research. *Journal of Occupational Health Psychology, 5*(2), 278-308.

Bakker, A. B., & Demerouti, E. (2008). Towards a model of work engagement. *Career Development International, 13*(3), 209-223.

Benioff, M., & Adler, C. (2019). *Trailblazer: The power of business as the greatest platform for change*. Currency.

Carlson, D. S., Grzywacz, J. G., & Zivnuska, S. (2009). Is work–family balance more than conflict and enrichment? *Human Relations, 62*(10), 1459-1486.

Deci, E. L., & Ryan, R. M. (2000). The "what" and "why" of goal pursuits: Human needs and the self-determination of behavior. *Psychological Inquiry, 11*(4), 227-268.

Greenhaus, J. H., & Beutell, N. J. (1985). Sources of conflict between work and family roles. *Academy of Management Review, 10*(1), 76-88.

Harter, J. K., Schmidt, F. L., & Hayes, T. L. (2002). Business-unit-level relationship between employee satisfaction, employee engagement, and business outcomes: A meta-analysis. *Journal of Applied Psychology, 87*(2), 268-279.

Hsieh, T. (2010). *Delivering happiness: A path to profits, passion, and purpose*. Business Plus.

Immelt, J. R. (2017). *Hot seat: What I learned leading a great American company*. Simon & Schuster.

Peters, J. (2019). *Employee engagement: Creating high positive energy at work*. Knowledge Resources.

Kossek, E. E., & Ozeki, C. (1998). Work–family conflict, policies, and the job–life satisfaction relationship: A review and directions for organizational behavior–human resources research. *Journal of Applied Psychology, 83*(2), 139-149.

Locke, E. A., & Latham, G. P. (2002). Building a practically useful theory of goal setting and task motivation: A 35-year odyssey. *American Psychologist, 57*(9), 705-717.

London, M., & Smither, J. W. (1999). Empowered self-development and continuous learning. *Human Resource Management, 38*(1), 3-15.

Macey, W. H., & Schneider, B. (2008). The meaning of employee engagement. *Industrial and Organizational Psychology, 1*(1), 3-30.

Nadella, S. (2017). *Hit refresh: The quest to rediscover Microsoft's soul and imagine a better future for everyone*. Harper Business.

Noe, R. A. (2017). *Employee training and development* (7th ed.). McGraw-Hill Education.

Roddick, A. (2005). *Business as unusual: My entrepreneurial journey, profits with principles*. Anita Roddick Books.

Saks, A. M. (2006). Antecedents and consequences of employee engagement. *Journal of Managerial Psychology, 21*(7), 600-619.

Schmidt, E., & Rosenberg, J. (2014). *How Google works*. Grand Central Publishing.

Chapter 7

Conflict Resolution and The Golden Rule

Conflict is an inevitable part of organizational life. Whether it's disagreements over strategies, differences in personalities, or competition for resources, conflicts can arise in any workplace. However, how conflicts are managed can significantly impact the organization's culture and performance. The Golden Rule—treating others as you would like to be treated—provides a powerful framework for resolving conflicts in a constructive and respectful manner. This chapter explores the strategies for conflict resolution through the lens of the Golden Rule, highlighting practical applications and real-world examples to demonstrate its effectiveness.

Understanding Conflict in the Workplace

Conflicts can arise for various reasons, including differences in values, goals, and perspectives. While conflicts are often perceived negatively, they can also provide opportunities for growth, innovation, and improved relationships if managed effectively.

Types of Workplace Conflicts

1. **Task Conflict**: Disagreements about the content and goals of the work. This type of conflict can be productive if it leads to better decision-making and innovative solutions (Jehn, 1995).

2. **Relationship Conflict**: Personal incompatibilities and tensions among individuals. This type of conflict is typically harmful as it can lead to stress, reduced cooperation, and lower productivity (Jehn, 1997).

3. Process Conflict: Disagreements about the methods and procedures used to complete tasks. While this conflict can sometimes be beneficial, it often leads to frustration and inefficiency if not managed properly (De Dreu & Weingart, 2003).

The Impact of Conflict

Unresolved conflicts can lead to a range of negative outcomes, including reduced productivity, low morale, increased absenteeism, and high turnover rates. On the other hand, effectively managed conflicts can foster creativity, improve team dynamics, and lead to better decision-making (De Dreu & Van Vianen, 2001).

The Golden Rule and Conflict Resolution

The Golden Rule—treating others as you would like to be treated—is a universal principle that can guide conflict resolution. By applying the Golden Rule, leaders and employees can approach conflicts with empathy, respect, and a commitment to finding mutually beneficial solutions.

Applying the Golden Rule to Conflict Resolution

1. Empathy and Understanding: Put yourself in the other person's shoes to understand their perspective and feelings. This empathy can help de-escalate tensions and foster a collaborative approach to resolving the conflict.

2. Respectful Communication: Communicate with respect and courtesy, even when disagreements arise. Avoid personal attacks, blame, and negative language.

3. Fairness and Equity: Strive for fair and equitable solutions that address the needs and concerns of all parties involved. Avoid favoritism and ensure that everyone is treated justly.

4. Collaboration and Compromise: Work together to find solutions that satisfy everyone's interests. Be willing to compromise and make concessions when necessary.

Case Study: Microsoft

Microsoft's approach to conflict resolution is guided by the principles of the Golden Rule. Under Satya Nadella's leadership, the company has emphasized empathy, respect, and collaboration in addressing conflicts. By fostering a culture of open communication and mutual respect, Microsoft has been able to resolve conflicts constructively, leading to improved team dynamics and innovation (Nadella, 2017).

Strategies for Effective Conflict Resolution

Effective conflict resolution requires a structured approach that incorporates the principles of the Golden Rule. The following strategies can help leaders and employees manage conflicts in a constructive and respectful manner:

1. Active Listening

Active listening involves fully concentrating, understanding, responding, and remembering what the other person is saying. This skill is crucial for understanding different perspectives and finding common ground.

- **Show Genuine Interest**: Pay full attention to the speaker, maintain eye contact, and avoid interrupting. Show that you are genuinely interested in understanding their perspective.

- **Reflect and Clarify**: Reflect on what you have heard to ensure understanding. Ask clarifying questions to get more details and avoid misunderstandings.

- **Acknowledge Emotions**: Recognize and acknowledge the speaker's emotions. This validation can help de-escalate tensions and build trust.

Case Study: Zappos

Zappos emphasizes active listening as a key component of its conflict resolution process. The company trains employees in active listening skills and encourages open communication to address conflicts. This approach has helped Zappos maintain a positive and collaborative work environment (Hsieh, 2010).

2. Open and Honest Communication

Open and honest communication is essential for resolving conflicts effectively. It involves expressing thoughts and feelings openly while also being respectful and considerate of others.

- **Be Transparent**: Share your thoughts and feelings honestly, but do so respectfully. Avoid hidden agendas and be upfront about your concerns and needs.

- **Use "I" Statements**: Use "I" statements to express your perspective without blaming or criticizing others. For example, say, "I feel concerned about…" instead of "You always…".

- **Stay Focused on the Issue**: Keep the conversation focused on the specific issue at hand. Avoid bringing up unrelated past conflicts or personal attacks.

Case Study: The Body Shop

The Body Shop encourages open and honest communication as part of its conflict resolution practices. The company's leadership promotes transparency and encourages employees to speak openly about their concerns. This approach has helped The Body Shop address conflicts constructively and maintain a respectful work environment (Roddick, 2005).

3. Collaborative Problem-Solving

Collaborative problem-solving involves working together to find solutions that meet the needs of all parties involved. This approach emphasizes cooperation, creativity, and mutual benefit.

- **Identify Common Goals**: Focus on common goals and shared interests. This can help shift the focus from individual positions to collective outcomes.

- **Generate Multiple Solutions**: Brainstorm multiple solutions to the conflict. Encourage creative thinking and consider various options before deciding on the best approach.

- **Evaluate and Choose the Best Solution**: Evaluate the potential solutions based on their feasibility, fairness, and ability to meet everyone's needs. Choose the solution that offers the most benefit to all parties.

Case Study: Patagonia

Patagonia uses collaborative problem-solving to address conflicts within the organization. The company's leaders facilitate discussions that focus on common goals and encourage creative solutions. This approach has helped Patagonia resolve conflicts constructively and maintain a positive work environment (Chouinard & Stanley, 2022).

4. Mediation and Third-Party Assistance

When conflicts cannot be resolved internally, mediation and third-party assistance can provide an impartial perspective and help facilitate resolution.

- **Use Trained Mediators**: Engage trained mediators who can facilitate discussions and help the parties find common ground. Mediators can provide an objective perspective and guide the resolution process.

- **Create Safe Spaces for Mediation**: Ensure that mediation sessions take place in a neutral and safe environment where all parties feel comfortable expressing their views.

- **Follow Structured Mediation Processes**: Use structured mediation processes that provide a clear framework for discussing the conflict and exploring solutions.

Case Study: Johnson & Johnson

Johnson & Johnson employs trained mediators to help resolve conflicts within the organization. The company's mediation processes emphasize fairness, respect, and collaboration, helping to address conflicts constructively and maintain a respectful work environment (Brenner, 2009).

5. Continuous Improvement and Follow-Up

Effective conflict resolution involves continuous improvement and follow-up to ensure that the solutions are working and that relationships are being repaired.

- **Monitor and Evaluate Outcomes**: Regularly monitor the outcomes of conflict resolution efforts to ensure that the solutions are effective and that the conflict has been resolved.

- **Provide Support and Resources**: Offer support and resources to help employees implement the agreed-upon solutions. This can include training, counseling, or additional mediation sessions if needed.

- **Encourage Continuous Feedback**: Encourage continuous feedback from employees about the conflict resolution process. Use this feedback to make improvements and address any ongoing issues.

Case Study: General Electric (GE)

General Electric emphasizes continuous improvement and follow-up in its conflict resolution practices. The company regularly evaluates the outcomes of conflict resolution efforts and provides support to ensure that solutions are effective. This approach has helped GE maintain a positive and productive work environment (Immelt, 2017).

Addressing DEI-Related Conflicts

Diversity, Equity, and Inclusion (DEI) initiatives can sometimes lead to conflicts in the workplace, particularly when there are differing opinions about the importance and implementation of these initiatives. Addressing DEI-related conflicts requires a sensitive and inclusive approach that balances the principles of the Golden Rule with the goals of DEI.

Understanding DEI-Related Conflicts

DEI-related conflicts can arise for various reasons, including resistance to change, perceived unfairness, and misunderstandings about the goals and benefits of DEI initiatives. These conflicts can be particularly challenging because they often involve deeply held beliefs and values.

Strategies for Addressing DEI-Related Conflicts

1. **Promote Education and Awareness**: Provide education and training about the importance of DEI and its benefits for the organization. Use real-world examples and case studies to illustrate how DEI can lead to better outcomes for everyone.

2. **Foster Inclusive Dialogue**: Create opportunities for open and respectful dialogue about DEI. Encourage employees to share their perspectives and experiences and listen actively to understand their concerns.

3. **Emphasize Common Goals**: Highlight the common goals and benefits of DEI initiatives, such as improved innovation, better decision-making, and a more inclusive work environment. Emphasize that DEI and merit are not mutually exclusive but can be integrated effectively.

4. **Address Concerns Fairly**: Take concerns about DEI initiatives seriously and address them fairly. Ensure that all employees feel heard and respected, and provide clear explanations about the goals and

implementation of DEI initiatives.

Case Study: IBM

IBM has successfully addressed DEI-related conflicts by promoting education and awareness, fostering inclusive dialogue, and emphasizing common goals. The company's leaders provide regular training on the importance of DEI, create opportunities for open dialogue, and address concerns fairly and transparently. This approach has helped IBM create an inclusive and respectful work environment (Rometty, 2019).

The Role of the Golden Rule in DEI-Related Conflicts

The Golden Rule can provide a valuable framework for addressing DEI-related conflicts. By treating others as you would like to be treated, leaders can create a respectful and inclusive environment where all employees feel valued and respected.

Applying the Golden Rule to DEI-Related Conflicts

1. **Empathy and Understanding**: Put yourself in the other person's shoes to understand their perspective and feelings about DEI initiatives. Show empathy and acknowledge their concerns.

2. **Respectful Communication**: Communicate with respect and courtesy, even when discussing sensitive or controversial topics. Avoid dismissive language and strive to understand different viewpoints.

3. **Fairness and Equity**: Ensure that DEI initiatives are implemented fairly and transparently. Avoid favoritism and ensure that all employees have equal access to opportunities and resources.

4. **Collaboration and Compromise**: Work together to find solutions that address everyone's concerns and promote a more inclusive work environment. Be willing to compromise and make concessions when necessary.

Case Study: Salesforce

Salesforce has applied the Golden Rule to address DEI-related conflicts within the organization. The company's leaders emphasize empathy, respect, and fairness in their approach to DEI, fostering an inclusive and supportive work environment. This approach has helped Salesforce address conflicts constructively and promote a culture of mutual respect (Benioff & Adler,

2019).

Conclusion

Conflict resolution is a critical skill for leaders and employees in any organization. By applying the Golden Rule—treating others as you would like to be treated—leaders can approach conflicts with empathy, respect, and a commitment to finding mutually beneficial solutions. Strategies such as active listening, open and honest communication, collaborative problem-solving, mediation, and continuous improvement can help resolve conflicts constructively and maintain a respectful work environment.

Addressing DEI-related conflicts requires a sensitive and inclusive approach that balances the principles of the Golden Rule with the goals of DEI. By promoting education and awareness, fostering inclusive dialogue, emphasizing common goals, and addressing concerns fairly, leaders can create an inclusive and high-performing work environment.

As we move forward in this book, we will continue to explore the profound implications of ethical leadership and the Golden Rule in various leadership contexts. We will delve into how these principles influence leadership behaviors, shape organizational cultures, and optimize operational effectiveness across diverse cultural landscapes. Through this exploration, we aim to provide deeper insights into the role of ethical leadership in fostering sustainable success and positive organizational climates.

References

Benioff, M., & Adler, C. (2019). *Trailblazer: The power of business as the greatest platform for change*. Currency.

Brenner, S. N. (2009). Johnson & Johnson's Credo: A corporate cultural relic or a practical guide to employees. *Journal of Business Ethics, 85*(3), 219-223.

Chouinard, Y., & Stanley, V. (2023). *The future of the responsible company: What we've learned from Patagonia's first 50 Years*. Patagonia.

De Dreu, C. K., & Van Vianen, A. E. (2001). Managing relationship conflict and the effectiveness of organizational teams. *Journal of Organizational Behavior: The International Journal of Industrial, Occupational and Organizational Psychology and Behavior, 22*(3), 309-328.

De Dreu, C. K., & Weingart, L. R. (2003). Task versus relationship conflict, team performance, and team member satisfaction: A meta-analysis. *Journal of Applied Psychology, 88*(4), 741-749.

Edmondson, A. (1999). Psychological safety and learning behavior in work teams. *Administrative Science Quarterly, 44*(2), 350-383.

Gelfand, M. J., Leslie, L. M., Keller, K. M., & de Dreu, C. K. (2012). Conflict cultures in organizations: How leaders shape conflict cultures and their organizational-level consequences. *Journal of Applied Psychology, 97*(6), 1131-1147.

Hsieh, T. (2010). *Delivering happiness: A path to profits, passion, and purpose.* Business Plus.

Immelt, J. R. (2017). *Hot seat: What I learned leading a great American company.* Simon & Schuster.

Jehn, K. A. (1995). A multimethod examination of the benefits and detriments of intragroup conflict. *Administrative Science Quarterly, 40*(2), 256-282.

Jehn, K. A. (1997). A qualitative analysis of conflict types and dimensions in organizational groups. *Administrative Science Quarterly, 42*(3), 530-557.

Johnson, L. (2022). *Global ethics and the environment: A leadership approach.* Springer.

Nadella, S. (2017). *Hit refresh: The quest to rediscover Microsoft's soul and imagine a better future for everyone.* Harper Business.

Roddick, A. (2005). *Business as unusual: My entrepreneurial journey, profits with principles.* Anita Roddick Books.

Rometty, G. (2019). *Good power: Leading positive change in our lives, work, and world.* Harvard Business Review Press.

Schmidt, E., & Rosenberg, J. (2014). *How Google works.* Grand Central Publishing.

Chapter 8

Leadership Styles and The Golden Rule

Effective leadership is crucial for the success and sustainability of any organization. Leadership styles significantly influence how leaders interact with their teams, make decisions, and drive organizational culture. The Golden Rule—treating others as you would like to be treated—can be a guiding principle that enhances various leadership styles, fostering a positive and productive work environment. This chapter explores different leadership styles, how the Golden Rule can be integrated into each, and the impact this integration has on organizational success.

Understanding Leadership Styles

Leadership styles refer to the behaviors and approaches leaders use to guide, motivate, and manage their teams. Different situations and organizational contexts may require different leadership styles, and effective leaders often adapt their style to meet the needs of their teams and achieve organizational goals.

1. Transformational Leadership

Transformational leadership involves inspiring and motivating employees to exceed their own interests for the sake of the organization. Transformational leaders are characterized by their ability to create a vision, communicate it effectively, and foster an environment that encourages innovation and change (Bass, 1985).

Integration of the Golden Rule

- **Empathy and Inspiration**: Transformational leaders can use the

Golden Rule to empathize with their team members, understanding their needs and aspirations. By treating employees as they would like to be treated, leaders can inspire and motivate their teams to achieve higher levels of performance.

- **Respect and Individual Consideration**: Transformational leaders should respect each team member's unique contributions and provide individualized support and recognition. This respect fosters a sense of belonging and commitment to the organization's vision.

Case Study: Steve Jobs at Apple

Steve Jobs, co-founder of Apple Inc., is often cited as a transformational leader. Jobs inspired his team by creating a compelling vision of innovation and excellence. By treating his team members with respect and valuing their creative contributions, Jobs fostered a culture of innovation that led to groundbreaking products and immense organizational success (Isaacson, 2011).

2. Servant Leadership

Servant leadership focuses on serving others, prioritizing the needs of employees, and fostering their development and well-being. Servant leaders lead by example and prioritize the growth and empowerment of their team members (Greenleaf, 1977).

Integration of the Golden Rule

- **Service and Empathy**: Servant leaders naturally align with the Golden Rule by prioritizing the needs and well-being of their team members. By treating employees with empathy and understanding, leaders can create a supportive and nurturing work environment.

- **Empowerment and Respect**: Servant leaders respect their team members' abilities and empower them to take initiative and make decisions. This empowerment fosters a sense of ownership and engagement among employees.

Case Study: Howard Schultz at Starbucks

Howard Schultz, former CEO of Starbucks, exemplifies servant leadership. Schultz focused on creating a supportive and inclusive workplace, offering comprehensive benefits and development opportunities for employees. By treating his team with respect and prioritizing their well-being, Schultz built a loyal and motivated workforce that contributed to Starbucks' global success (Schultz & Yang, 2011).

3. Transactional Leadership

Transactional leadership is based on a system of rewards and penalties. Transactional leaders focus on maintaining routine operations and ensuring that employees meet specific performance standards and objectives (Burns, 1978).

Integration of the Golden Rule

• **Fairness and Integrity**: Transactional leaders can integrate the Golden Rule by ensuring that rewards and penalties are applied fairly and consistently. Treating employees with fairness and integrity helps build trust and accountability within the team.

• **Recognition and Respect**: Recognizing and rewarding employees' efforts and achievements shows respect for their contributions. This recognition can motivate employees to perform at their best and adhere to organizational standards.

Case Study: GE Under Jack Welch

Jack Welch, former CEO of General Electric, is known for his transactional leadership style. Welch implemented a performance-based system that rewarded high achievers and addressed underperformance. By treating employees fairly and recognizing their contributions, Welch drove GE to become one of the most successful companies in the world (Welch & Welch, 2005).

4. Democratic Leadership

Democratic leadership, also known as participative leadership, involves including team members in decision-making processes. Democratic leaders value collaboration and seek input from employees before making decisions (Lewin, Lippitt, & White, 1939).

Integration of the Golden Rule

• **Inclusivity and Respect**: Democratic leaders can apply the Golden Rule by valuing employees' opinions and involving them in decision-making. This inclusivity and respect for diverse perspectives foster a collaborative and engaged workforce.

- **Transparency and Fairness**: By being transparent about decisions and ensuring that all voices are heard, democratic leaders build trust and accountability. Treating employees with fairness and respect during the decision-making process enhances their commitment to organizational goals.

Case Study: Google's Management Style

Google's management style emphasizes democratic leadership, encouraging employees to participate in decision-making and innovation processes. By treating employees as valuable contributors and respecting their input, Google has created a culture of collaboration and innovation that drives its success (Schmidt & Rosenberg, 2014).

5. Autocratic Leadership

Autocratic leadership involves making decisions unilaterally and maintaining strict control over the team. Autocratic leaders provide clear direction and expect employees to follow instructions without input or feedback (Lewin, Lippitt, & White, 1939).

Integration of the Golden Rule

- **Clarity and Respect**: While autocratic leadership may seem at odds with the Golden Rule, leaders can still treat employees with respect by providing clear and consistent direction. Respecting employees' need for clarity and stability can enhance their performance and job satisfaction.

- **Fairness and Accountability**: Autocratic leaders should apply the Golden Rule by ensuring that their decisions are fair and that they hold themselves accountable to the same standards they set for their team. This fairness and accountability build trust and respect among employees.

Case Study: Bill Gates at Microsoft

Bill Gates, co-founder of Microsoft, often employed an autocratic leadership style during the company's early years. Gates provided clear direction and maintained strict control over decision-making processes. By treating employees with respect and fairness, Gates was able to drive innovation and establish Microsoft as a leading technology company

(Wallace & Erickson, 1992).

The Impact of Integrating the Golden Rule into Leadership Styles

Integrating the Golden Rule into various leadership styles can have a profound impact on organizational culture, employee engagement, and overall performance. By treating employees with empathy, respect, and fairness, leaders can foster a positive and productive work environment that drives success.

1. Enhanced Employee Engagement

When leaders treat employees with respect and fairness, it enhances their engagement and commitment to the organization. Engaged employees are more motivated, productive, and willing to go above and beyond to achieve organizational goals (Peters, 2019).

2. Improved Team Collaboration

Applying the Golden Rule fosters a culture of collaboration and mutual respect. Employees are more likely to work together effectively, share ideas, and support each other in achieving common objectives (Edmondson, 1999).

3. Higher Job Satisfaction and Retention

Employees who feel valued and respected by their leaders are more satisfied with their jobs and less likely to leave the organization. High job satisfaction and retention rates contribute to a stable and experienced workforce (Spector, 2022).

4. Better Decision-Making

Leaders who involve employees in decision-making and value their input make better-informed decisions. This collaborative approach leverages diverse perspectives and expertise, leading to more effective solutions (Vroom & Jago, 1988).

5. Positive Organizational Culture

Integrating the Golden Rule into leadership styles helps build a positive organizational culture based on trust, respect, and ethical behavior. This positive culture enhances the organization's reputation and attracts top talent (Schein, 2010).

Practical Applications and Real-World Examples

The following real-world examples illustrate how integrating the Golden Rule into various leadership styles can drive organizational success:

Case Study: Google

Google's democratic leadership style and commitment to treating employees with respect and inclusivity have fostered a culture of innovation and collaboration. By involving employees in decision-making and valuing their contributions, Google has maintained high levels of engagement and productivity, driving its success in the technology industry (Schmidt & Rosenberg, 2014).

Case Study: Starbucks

Howard Schultz's servant leadership at Starbucks has created a supportive and inclusive work environment. By prioritizing the well-being of employees and treating them with empathy and respect, Schultz built a loyal and motivated workforce that contributed to Starbucks' global success (Schultz & Yang, 2011).

Case Study: General Electric

Jack Welch's transactional leadership at General Electric emphasized fairness and accountability. By treating employees with respect and recognizing their achievements, Welch drove GE to become one of the most successful companies in the world (Welch & Welch, 2005).

Case Study: Apple

Steve Jobs' transformational leadership at Apple inspired innovation and excellence. By respecting employees' creative contributions and treating them with fairness, Jobs fostered a culture of innovation that led to groundbreaking products and immense organizational success (Isaacson, 2011).

Case Study: Microsoft

Bill Gates' autocratic leadership at Microsoft provided clear direction and stability during the company's early years. By treating employees with respect and fairness, Gates was able to drive innovation and establish Microsoft as a leading technology company (Wallace & Erickson, 1992).

Conclusion

Leadership styles significantly influence organizational culture, employee engagement, and overall performance. By integrating the Golden Rule—treating others as you would like to be treated—into various leadership styles, leaders can enhance their effectiveness and foster a positive and productive work environment.

The benefits of applying the Golden Rule to leadership are clear: enhanced employee engagement, improved team collaboration, higher job satisfaction and retention, better decision-making, and a positive organizational culture. Through the strategies and real-world examples presented in this chapter, leaders can gain valuable insights into how to apply the Golden Rule to their leadership style and drive organizational success.

As we move forward in this book, we will continue to explore the profound implications of ethical leadership and the Golden Rule in various leadership contexts. We will delve into how these principles influence leadership behaviors, shape organizational cultures, and optimize operational effectiveness across diverse cultural landscapes. Through this exploration, we aim to provide deeper insights into the role of ethical leadership in fostering sustainable success and positive organizational climates.

References

Bass, B. M. (1985). *Leadership and performance beyond expectations.* Free Press.

Burns, J. M. (1978). *Leadership.* Harper & Row.

Edmondson, A. (1999). Psychological safety and learning behavior in work teams. *Administrative Science Quarterly, 44*(2), 350-383.

Greenleaf, R. K. (1977). *Servant leadership: A journey into the nature of legitimate power and greatness.* Paulist Press.

Isaacson, W. (2011). *Steve Jobs.* Simon & Schuster.

Peters, J. (2019). *Employee engagement: Creating high positive energy at work.* Knowledge Resources.

Lewin, K., Lippitt, R., & White, R. K. (1939). Patterns of aggressive behavior in experimentally created social climates. *The Journal of Social Psychology, 10*(2), 271-299.

Spector, P. E. (2022). *Job satisfaction: From assessment to intervention.* Routledge.

Nadella, S. (2017). *Hit refresh: The quest to rediscover Microsoft's soul and imagine a better future for everyone.* Harper Business.

Roddick, A. (2005). *Business as unusual: My entrepreneurial journey, profits with principles.* Anita Roddick Books.

Schmidt, E., & Rosenberg, J. (2014). *How Google works.* Grand Central Publishing.

Schein, E. H. (2010). *Organizational culture and leadership* (4th ed.). Jossey-Bass.

Schultz, H., & Yang, D. J. (2011). *Onward: How Starbucks fought for its life without losing its soul.* Rodale Books.

Vroom, V. H., & Jago, A. G. (1988). *The new leadership: Managing participation in organizations.* Prentice-Hall.

Wallace, J., & Erickson, J. (1992). *Hard drive: Bill Gates and the making of the Microsoft empire.* Harper Business.

Welch, J., & Welch, S. (2005). *Winning.* Harper Business.

Chapter 9

Ethical Decision-Making and the Golden Rule

In the ever-evolving landscape of modern business, ethical decision-making stands as a cornerstone of successful and sustainable leadership. The Golden Rule—treating others as you would like to be treated—provides a timeless and universal framework for making ethical decisions. This chapter delves into the principles of ethical decision-making, explores how the Golden Rule can guide leaders in navigating complex ethical dilemmas, and presents real-world examples to illustrate the application of these principles in organizational contexts.

Understanding Ethical Decision Making

Ethical decision-making involves choosing actions that are morally right and that promote the well-being of individuals and the organization. It requires leaders to consider the impact of their decisions on various stakeholders, including employees, customers, shareholders, and the broader community.

Principles of Ethical Decision Making

1. **Integrity**: Acting with honesty and transparency in all dealings.

2. **Fairness**: Ensuring that decisions are just and impartial.

3. **Accountability**: Taking responsibility for the consequences of decisions.

4. **Respect**: Valuing the dignity and rights of all individuals.

5. **Empathy**: Understanding and considering the perspectives and

feelings of others.

The Role of Ethical Frameworks

Ethical frameworks provide structured approaches to decision-making that help leaders evaluate their options and choose the most ethical course of action. Common ethical frameworks include utilitarianism (focusing on the greatest good for the greatest number), deontology (focusing on duties and principles), and virtue ethics (focusing on moral character and virtues).

The Golden Rule as an Ethical Framework

The Golden Rule serves as a simple yet powerful ethical framework that transcends cultural and religious boundaries. By considering how one would like to be treated in a similar situation, leaders can make decisions that are fair, compassionate, and respectful.

Applying the Golden Rule to Ethical Decision-Making

1. **Empathy and Understanding**: Put yourself in the shoes of those affected by the decision. Consider their perspectives, needs, and concerns.

2. **Respect and Dignity**: Ensure that the decision respects the dignity and rights of all individuals involved.

3. **Fairness and Justice**: Strive for fairness by treating all parties equitably and justly.

4. **Transparency and Honesty**: Communicate openly and honestly about the decision-making process and its outcomes.

5. **Accountability and Responsibility**: Take responsibility for the consequences of the decision and be willing to make amends if necessary.

Case Study: Johnson & Johnson's Tylenol Crisis

Johnson & Johnson's response to the Tylenol crisis in 1982 is a classic example of applying the Golden Rule to ethical decision-making. When it was discovered that Tylenol capsules had been tampered with and laced with cyanide, resulting in several deaths, the company's leadership faced a critical ethical dilemma.

Applying the principles of the Golden Rule, Johnson & Johnson's leaders prioritized the safety and well-being of their customers. They promptly recalled all Tylenol products from the market, even though it resulted in significant financial loss. The company communicated openly with the public, providing transparent updates on the situation and the steps being taken to address it. By treating their customers with respect, fairness, and empathy, Johnson & Johnson not only mitigated the crisis but also strengthened its reputation for ethical leadership (Brenner, 2009).

Strategies for Ethical Decision Making

Ethical decision-making requires a deliberate and thoughtful approach. The following strategies can help leaders integrate the Golden Rule into their decision-making processes:

1. Establish Clear Ethical Guidelines

Developing and implementing clear ethical guidelines provides a foundation for consistent and principled decision-making.

- **Create a Code of Ethics**: Develop a comprehensive code of ethics that outlines the organization's values, principles, and expectations for ethical behavior. Ensure that all employees are familiar with and adhere to these guidelines.

- **Provide Ethics Training**: Offer regular training programs to educate employees about ethical decision-making and the importance of the Golden Rule. Use real-world scenarios and case studies to illustrate key concepts.

- **Promote Ethical Leadership**: Encourage leaders at all levels to model ethical behavior and decision-making. Recognize and reward leaders who demonstrate a strong commitment to ethics.

Case Study: General Electric

General Electric (GE) has established a robust ethical framework through its code of conduct, which emphasizes integrity, fairness, and accountability. GE provides regular ethics training and promotes ethical leadership by recognizing leaders who exemplify ethical decision-making. This commitment to ethics has helped GE maintain a strong reputation for integrity and responsible business practices (Immelt, 2017).

2. Foster an Ethical Organizational Culture

An ethical organizational culture supports and reinforces ethical decision-making by embedding ethical values and principles into the organization's daily operations and practices.

- **Encourage Open Dialogue**: Create an environment where employees feel comfortable discussing ethical concerns and dilemmas. Encourage open and honest communication about ethics.

- **Support Whistleblowing**: Implement mechanisms that allow employees to report unethical behavior without fear of retaliation. Ensure that whistleblowers are protected and their concerns are addressed promptly.

- **Integrate Ethics into Performance Evaluations**: Include ethical behavior and decision-making as key criteria in performance evaluations. Hold employees accountable for adhering to the organization's ethical standards.

Case Study: The Body Shop

The Body Shop has fostered an ethical organizational culture by promoting open dialogue about ethical issues and supporting whistleblowing. The company's leadership integrates ethics into performance evaluations, ensuring that ethical behavior is recognized and rewarded. This culture of ethics has helped The Body Shop maintain its commitment to social responsibility and sustainability (Roddick, 2005).

3. Engage Stakeholders in Decision Making

Engaging stakeholders in the decision-making process ensures that diverse perspectives are considered and that decisions are made transparently and inclusively.

- **Identify Key Stakeholders**: Identify all stakeholders who may be affected by the decision, including employees, customers, shareholders, and the community.

- **Solicit Input and Feedback**: Actively seek input and feedback from stakeholders. Use surveys, focus groups, and public consultations to gather diverse perspectives.

- **Communicate Transparently**: Keep stakeholders informed about the decision-making process and its outcomes. Provide clear and honest communication about the reasons behind decisions.

Case Study: Patagonia

Patagonia engages stakeholders in its decision-making process by soliciting input and feedback from employees, customers, and environmental organizations. The company's leadership communicates transparently about its sustainability initiatives and ethical practices. This stakeholder engagement has helped Patagonia build trust and loyalty among its stakeholders and reinforce its commitment to ethical business practices (Chouinard & Stanley, 2022).

4. Implement a Decision-Making Framework

A structured decision-making framework helps leaders evaluate options systematically and choose the most ethical course of action.

- **Define the Problem**: Clearly define the ethical dilemma or decision to be made. Identify the key issues and stakeholders involved.

- **Gather Information**: Collect relevant information and data to understand the context and implications of the decision. Consider the perspectives and needs of all stakeholders.

- **Evaluate Options**: Assess the potential options and their impact on stakeholders. Use ethical frameworks, such as the Golden Rule, to evaluate the fairness, respect, and integrity of each option.

- **Make the Decision**: Choose the option that aligns with the organization's ethical values and principles. Ensure that the decision is fair, transparent, and respectful to all parties involved.

- **Implement and Monitor**: Implement the decision and monitor its impact. Be prepared to make adjustments if necessary and take responsibility for the outcomes.

Case Study: Google

Google uses a structured decision-making framework to address ethical dilemmas and ensure that decisions align with the company's values. The framework involves defining the problem, gathering information, evaluating options, making the decision, and monitoring the outcomes. By applying this framework, Google has been able to navigate complex ethical issues and maintain its commitment to ethical leadership (Schmidt & Rosenberg, 2014).

The Role of Leadership in Ethical Decision Making

Leaders play a critical role in promoting and modeling ethical decision-making within their organizations. By integrating the Golden Rule into their leadership practices, leaders can foster a culture of ethics and integrity that drives sustainable success.

1. Leading by Example

Leaders set the tone for ethical behavior through their actions and decisions. By demonstrating a commitment to the Golden Rule, leaders can inspire their teams to act ethically and responsibly.

- **Model Ethical Behavior**: Act with integrity, fairness, and respect in all interactions. Show empathy and understanding towards others.

- **Be Transparent and Honest**: Communicate openly and honestly about decisions and their rationale. Ensure that your actions align with your words.

- **Take Responsibility**: Be accountable for your decisions and their impact. Acknowledge mistakes and take corrective actions when necessary.

Case Study: Howard Schultz at Starbucks

Howard Schultz, former CEO of Starbucks, led by example by demonstrating a strong commitment to ethical behavior. Schultz prioritized transparency, honesty, and accountability in his leadership, fostering a culture of trust and integrity at Starbucks. This ethical leadership has been instrumental in Starbucks' success and reputation (Schultz & Yang, 2011).

2. Encouraging Ethical Behavior

Leaders can encourage ethical behavior by creating an environment that supports and rewards ethical decision-making.

- **Recognize and Reward Ethics**: Recognize and reward employees who demonstrate ethical behavior and decision-making. Highlight their contributions and set them as examples for others to follow.

- **Provide Ethical Resources**: Offer resources, such as ethics training and decision-making tools, to help employees navigate ethical dilemmas. Provide guidance and support for ethical decision-making.

- **Foster a Supportive Culture**: Create a culture where ethical behavior is valued and supported. Encourage open discussions about ethics and provide a safe space for employees to voice their concerns.

Case Study: Microsoft

Microsoft encourages ethical behavior by recognizing and rewarding employees who demonstrate ethical decision-making. The company provides extensive resources, including ethics training and decision-making frameworks, to support employees in making ethical choices. This commitment to ethics has helped Microsoft build a strong reputation for integrity and responsible business practices (Nadella, 2017).

3. Building Ethical Capacity

Leaders can build ethical capacity within their organizations by developing employees' ethical decision-making skills and fostering a culture of continuous learning and improvement.

- **Offer Ethics Training**: Provide regular training programs that focus on ethical decision-making, the Golden Rule, and the organization's values and principles. Use real-world scenarios and case studies to illustrate key concepts.

- **Encourage Continuous Learning**: Promote a culture of continuous learning and improvement. Encourage employees to seek out new knowledge and skills related to ethics and responsible leadership.

- **Support Ethical Development**: Provide opportunities for employees to develop their ethical decision-making skills. Offer mentorship, coaching, and development programs that focus on ethics and integrity.

Case Study: General Electric

General Electric builds ethical capacity within the organization by offering regular ethics training and development programs. The company encourages continuous learning and provides support for employees to develop their ethical decision-making skills. This commitment to building ethical capacity has helped GE maintain a strong reputation for integrity and responsible leadership (Immelt, 2017).

Conclusion

Ethical decision-making is a critical component of successful and sustainable leadership. By applying the Golden Rule—treating others as you would like to be treated—leaders can navigate complex ethical dilemmas with empathy, respect, and fairness. The principles of ethical decision-making, including integrity, fairness, accountability, respect, and empathy, provide a foundation for making morally right and responsible choices.

The strategies for ethical decision-making, such as establishing clear ethical guidelines, fostering an ethical organizational culture, engaging stakeholders, and implementing a structured decision-making framework, help leaders integrate the Golden Rule into their leadership practices. By leading by example, encouraging ethical behavior, and building ethical capacity, leaders can create a culture of ethics and integrity that drives organizational success.

As we move forward in this book, we will continue to explore the profound implications of ethical leadership and the Golden Rule in various leadership contexts. We will delve into how these principles influence leadership behaviors, shape organizational cultures, and optimize operational effectiveness across diverse cultural landscapes. Through this exploration, we aim to provide deeper insights into the role of ethical leadership in fostering sustainable success and positive organizational climates.

References

Brenner, S. N. (2009). Johnson & Johnson's Credo: A corporate cultural relic or a practical guide to employees. *Journal of Business Ethics, 85*(3), 219-223.

Chouinard, Y., & Stanley, V. (2023). *The future of the responsible company: What we've learned from Patagonia's first 50 Years*. Patagonia.

Greenleaf, R. K. (1977). *Servant leadership: A journey into the nature of legitimate power and greatness*. Paulist Press.

Immelt, J. R. (2017). *Hot seat: What I learned leading a great American company*. Simon & Schuster.

Isaacson, W. (2011). *Steve Jobs*. Simon & Schuster.

Nadella, S. (2017). *Hit refresh: The quest to rediscover Microsoft's soul and imagine a better future for everyone*. Harper Business.

Roddick, A. (2005). *Business as unusual: My entrepreneurial journey, profits with principles*. Anita Roddick Books.

Schmidt, E., & Rosenberg, J. (2014). *How Google works*. Grand Central Publishing.

Schultz, H., & Yang, D. J. (2011). *Onward: How Starbucks fought for its life without losing its soul*. Rodale Books.

Chapter 10

Building Trust and Accountability in Leadership

Trust and accountability are foundational elements of effective leadership and organizational success. Leaders who prioritize these principles foster a positive work environment, enhance employee engagement, and drive sustainable performance. The Golden Rule—treating others as you would like to be treated—serves as a guiding principle for building trust and accountability in leadership. This chapter explores the importance of trust and accountability, provides strategies for leaders to cultivate these qualities, and presents real-world examples to illustrate their impact on organizational culture and success.

Understanding Trust and Accountability in Leadership

Trust is the belief in the reliability, integrity, and competence of an individual or organization. It is built through consistent actions that demonstrate honesty, transparency, and ethical behavior. Accountability involves taking responsibility for one's actions and decisions and being answerable to others for the outcomes.

The Importance of Trust

Trust is essential for effective leadership and organizational performance. It fosters a collaborative and supportive work environment, enhances communication, and drives employee engagement and motivation.

1. **Enhanced Collaboration**: Trust encourages open communication and collaboration among team members. Employees are more willing to

share ideas, take risks, and work together towards common goals (Costa, Roe, & Taillieu, 2001).

2. Increased Engagement: Trust in leadership boosts employee engagement and commitment. Engaged employees are more motivated, productive, and loyal to the organization (Dirks & Ferrin, 2002).

3. Better Decision-Making: Trust enables leaders to make informed decisions with the support and input of their team. It fosters a culture where diverse perspectives are valued and considered (McEvily, Perrone, & Zaheer, 2003).

The Importance of Accountability

Accountability ensures that individuals and teams are responsible for their actions and outcomes. It promotes a culture of ownership, continuous improvement, and ethical behavior.

1. Improved Performance: Accountability drives performance by setting clear expectations and holding individuals responsible for meeting them. It encourages continuous improvement and excellence (Tate et al., 2022).

2. Ethical Behavior: Accountability reinforces ethical behavior by ensuring that individuals are answerable for their actions. It deters misconduct and promotes integrity and transparency (Yusnai, 2022).

3. Organizational Trust: Accountability builds trust within the organization by demonstrating that leaders and employees are committed to ethical standards and responsible conduct (Robinson, 1996).

The Role of the Golden Rule in Building Trust and Accountability

The Golden Rule provides a simple yet profound framework for fostering trust and accountability in leadership. By treating others as you would like to be treated, leaders can build trust, demonstrate accountability, and create a positive organizational culture.

Applying the Golden Rule to Build Trust

1. Honesty and Transparency: Be honest and transparent in all communications and actions. Share information openly and truthfully, and admit mistakes when they occur.

2. Consistency and Reliability: Demonstrate consistency and reliability in your actions. Follow through on commitments and promises, and be dependable in your leadership.

3. Respect and Empathy: Treat employees with respect and empathy. Show genuine concern for their well-being and listen to their perspectives and needs.

Applying the Golden Rule to Demonstrate Accountability

1. Take Responsibility: Accept responsibility for your actions and decisions. Be willing to acknowledge mistakes and take corrective actions when necessary.

2. Set Clear Expectations: Clearly communicate expectations and standards to your team. Ensure that everyone understands their roles and responsibilities.

3. Provide Constructive Feedback: Offer constructive feedback to help employees improve and grow. Recognize achievements and address performance issues fairly and respectfully.

Case Study: Microsoft

Under the leadership of Satya Nadella, Microsoft has prioritized trust and accountability. Nadella's commitment to honesty, transparency, and empathy has built trust among employees and stakeholders. By setting clear expectations and taking responsibility for the company's direction, Nadella has fostered a culture of accountability that drives performance and innovation (Nadella, 2017).

Strategies for Building Trust in Leadership

Building trust requires consistent and intentional efforts from leaders. The following strategies can help leaders cultivate trust within their teams and organizations:

1. Foster Open Communication

Open communication is essential for building trust. Leaders should create an environment where employees feel comfortable sharing their ideas, concerns, and feedback.

- **Encourage Open Dialogue**: Hold regular meetings and forums where employees can voice their opinions and ask questions. Ensure that these discussions are respectful and inclusive.

- **Listen Actively**: Practice active listening by giving employees your full attention, acknowledging their input, and responding thoughtfully. This demonstrates that you value their contributions.

- **Be Transparent**: Share information openly and honestly with employees. Provide updates on organizational goals, challenges, and developments.

Case Study: Google

Google's open communication culture is a key factor in building trust within the organization. The company encourages open dialogue through regular town hall meetings, Q&A sessions with executives, and internal communication platforms. This transparency fosters trust and collaboration among employees (Schmidt & Rosenberg, 2014).

2. Demonstrate Integrity and Ethical Behavior

Integrity and ethical behavior are fundamental to building trust. Leaders should model these qualities in their actions and decisions.

- **Act with Integrity**: Be honest and ethical in all dealings. Keep promises and adhere to the organization's values and principles.

- **Address Ethical Issues Promptly**: Address any ethical issues or misconduct promptly and fairly. Ensure that the organization's ethical standards are upheld.

- **Promote a Culture of Ethics**: Foster a culture where ethical behavior is valued and recognized. Encourage employees to act with integrity and hold them accountable for ethical conduct.

Case Study: Johnson & Johnson

Johnson & Johnson's commitment to integrity and ethical behavior is exemplified by its response to the Tylenol crisis in 1982. The company's leaders prioritized customer safety and transparency, building trust and reinforcing the company's reputation for ethical leadership (Brenner, 2009).

3. Build Relationships and Rapport

Building strong relationships and rapport with employees fosters trust and mutual respect. Leaders should take the time to connect with their team members on a personal level.

- **Show Genuine Interest**: Take an interest in employees' lives and well-being. Get to know them as individuals and build personal connections.

- **Be Approachable**: Make yourself approachable and accessible to employees. Encourage them to come to you with their ideas, concerns, and questions.

- **Recognize and Appreciate**: Recognize and appreciate employees' efforts and achievements. Show gratitude for their contributions and celebrate their successes.

Case Study: Starbucks

Howard Schultz's leadership at Starbucks is characterized by strong relationships and rapport with employees. Schultz's genuine interest in employees' well-being and his approachable leadership style have built trust and loyalty within the organization (Schultz & Yang, 2011).

4. Empower and Support Employees

Empowering and supporting employees builds trust by demonstrating that leaders have confidence in their abilities and are committed to their growth and development.

- **Delegate Responsibility**: Delegate responsibilities and tasks to employees, giving them the autonomy to make decisions and take ownership of their work.

- **Provide Resources and Support**: Ensure that employees have the resources and support they need to succeed. Offer training, tools, and guidance to help them achieve their goals.

- **Encourage Growth and Development**: Support employees' professional growth and development by providing opportunities for learning and advancement. Encourage them to pursue their career aspirations.

Case Study: Patagonia

Patagonia's leadership empowers and supports employees by delegating responsibility and providing resources for growth and development. The company's commitment to employee empowerment has built trust and fostered a positive work environment (Chouinard & Stanley, 2022).

Strategies for Demonstrating Accountability in Leadership

Demonstrating accountability requires leaders to take responsibility for their actions and decisions and to ensure that their team members do the same. The following strategies can help leaders foster a culture of accountability:

1. Set Clear Expectations and Goals

Setting clear expectations and goals provides a foundation for accountability. Leaders should communicate these expectations and ensure that everyone understands their roles and responsibilities.

- **Define Roles and Responsibilities**: Clearly define each team member's roles and responsibilities. Ensure that everyone knows what is expected of them.

- **Set SMART Goals**: Establish specific, measurable, achievable, relevant, and time-bound (SMART) goals. Ensure that these goals align with the organization's objectives.

- **Monitor Progress**: Regularly monitor progress towards goals and provide feedback. Adjust expectations as needed to ensure that goals remain relevant and attainable.

Case Study: General Electric

Jack Welch's leadership at General Electric emphasized setting clear expectations and goals. Welch implemented a performance-based system that defined roles, set SMART goals, and monitored progress. This approach fostered a culture of accountability and drove GE's success (Welch & Welch, 2005).

2. Hold Yourself and Others Accountable

Leaders should model accountability by taking responsibility for their actions and holding others accountable for theirs.

- **Acknowledge Mistakes**: Admit mistakes and take responsibility for them. Show employees that it is acceptable to make mistakes as long as they learn from them.

- **Provide Constructive Feedback**: Offer constructive feedback to help employees improve and grow. Address performance issues fairly and respectfully.

- **Recognize Achievements**: Recognize and reward employees who demonstrate accountability and achieve their goals. Highlight their contributions and set them as examples for others.

Case Study: IBM

IBM's leadership emphasizes accountability by holding themselves and their team members responsible for their actions and outcomes. The company provides constructive feedback and recognizes achievements, fostering a culture of accountability and continuous improvement (Rometty, 2019).

3. Create a Culture of Continuous Improvement

A culture of continuous improvement encourages employees to take responsibility for their performance and strive for excellence.

- **Encourage Learning and Development**: Promote a culture of continuous learning and development. Encourage employees to seek out new knowledge and skills.

- **Foster Innovation and Experimentation**: Create an environment where employees feel comfortable experimenting and innovating. Support their efforts to find new and better ways of doing things.

- **Celebrate Progress and Success**: Celebrate progress and success, no matter how small. Recognize and reward employees' efforts to improve and achieve their goals.

Case Study: Google

Google fosters a culture of continuous improvement by encouraging learning, development, and innovation. The company's leadership supports experimentation and celebrates progress, driving accountability and excellence (Schmidt & Rosenberg, 2014).

4. Ensure Fairness and Equity

Fairness and equity are essential for fostering accountability. Leaders should ensure that expectations and standards are applied consistently and fairly.

- **Apply Standards Consistently**: Apply expectations and standards consistently to all employees. Avoid favoritism and ensure that everyone is held to the same standards.

- **Address Issues Fairly**: Address performance issues and misconduct fairly and objectively. Ensure that any consequences are appropriate and just.

- **Promote Equity and Inclusion**: Promote equity and inclusion by ensuring that all employees have equal access to opportunities and resources. Create an inclusive environment where everyone feels valued and respected.

Case Study: Microsoft

Microsoft promotes fairness and equity through its commitment to diversity and inclusion. The company's leadership ensures that expectations and standards are applied consistently and that all employees have equal access to opportunities. This commitment to fairness and equity fosters accountability and trust (Nadella, 2017).

Real-World Applications and Benefits

The following real-world examples illustrate the impact of trust and accountability on organizational success:

Case Study: Google

Google's commitment to open communication, transparency, and continuous improvement has built trust and accountability within the organization. By fostering a culture where employees feel valued and supported, Google has maintained high levels of engagement and innovation, driving its success in the technology industry (Schmidt & Rosenberg, 2014).

Case Study: Starbucks

Howard Schultz's leadership at Starbucks emphasizes trust, empathy, and accountability. Schultz's genuine interest in employees' well-being and his commitment to ethical behavior have built trust and loyalty within the organization. This trust has been instrumental in Starbucks' global success and reputation (Schultz & Yang, 2011).

Case Study: General Electric

Jack Welch's leadership at General Electric focused on setting clear expectations, providing constructive feedback, and recognizing achievements. This approach fostered a culture of accountability and continuous improvement, driving GE to become one of the most successful companies in the world (Welch & Welch, 2005).

Case Study: Patagonia

Patagonia's leadership empowers and supports employees by delegating responsibility and providing resources for growth and development. The company's commitment to employee empowerment and ethical behavior has built trust and fostered a positive work environment, contributing to Patagonia's success and reputation (Chouinard & Stanley, 2022).

Conclusion

Trust and accountability are essential components of effective leadership and organizational success. By applying the Golden Rule—treating others as you would like to be treated—leaders can build trust, demonstrate accountability, and create a positive organizational culture.

The strategies for building trust, such as fostering open communication, demonstrating integrity, building relationships, and empowering employees, help leaders cultivate trust within their teams and organizations. The strategies for demonstrating accountability, such as setting clear expectations, holding oneself and others accountable, creating a culture of continuous improvement, and ensuring fairness and equity, help leaders foster a culture of accountability.

The benefits of trust and accountability are clear: enhanced collaboration, increased engagement, better decision-making, improved performance, ethical behavior, and a positive organizational culture. Through the strategies and real-world examples presented in this chapter, leaders can gain valuable insights into how to build trust and demonstrate accountability in their leadership practices.

As we conclude this book, we hope to have provided deeper insights into the role of ethical leadership and the Golden Rule in fostering sustainable success and positive organizational climates. By integrating these principles into their leadership practices, leaders can drive organizational success, create a positive impact on their teams and communities, and leave a lasting legacy of ethical leadership.

References

Tate, D. C., Pantalon, M. S., & David, D. H. (2022). *Conscious accountability: Deepen connections, elevate results.* Association for Talent Development. .

Brenner, S. N. (2009). Johnson & Johnson's Credo: A corporate cultural relic or a practical guide to employees. *Journal of Business Ethics, 85*(3), 219-223.

Chouinard, Y., & Stanley, V. (2023). *The future of the responsible company: What we've learned from Patagonia's first 50 Years.* Patagonia.

Costa, A. C., Roe, R. A., & Taillieu, T. (2001). Trust within teams: The relation with performance effectiveness. *European Journal of Work and Organizational Psychology, 10*(3), 225-244.

Dirks, K. T., & Ferrin, D. L. (2002). Trust in leadership: Meta-analytic findings and implications for research and practice. *Journal of Applied Psychology, 87*(4), 611-628.

McEvily, B., Perrone, V., & Zaheer, A. (2003). Trust as an organizing principle. *Organization Science, 14*(1), 91-103.

Nadella, S. (2017). *Hit refresh: The quest to rediscover Microsoft's soul and imagine a better future for everyone.* Harper Business.

Robinson, S. L. (1996). Trust and breach of the psychological contract. *Administrative Science Quarterly, 41*(4), 574-599.

Roddick, A. (2005). *Business as unusual: My entrepreneurial journey, profits with principles.* Anita Roddick Books.

Rometty, G. (2019). *Good power: Leading positive change in our lives, work, and world*. Harvard Business Review Press.

Yusnaini Yusnaini. (2023). Triangle Model of Responsibility Theory in Perspective of Internal Auditor's Responsibility for Fraud Detection. *International Journal of Economic Behavior and Organization, 11*(3), 146-153.

Schmidt, E., & Rosenberg, J. (2014). *How Google works*. Grand Central Publishing.

Schultz, H., & Yang, D. J. (2011). *Onward: How Starbucks fought for its life without losing its soul*. Rodale Books.

Welch, J., & Welch, S. (2005). *Winning*. Harper Business.

Chapter 11

Inspiring Innovation and Creativity through the Golden Rule

In the dynamic and competitive landscape of modern business, innovation and creativity are essential for organizational success and sustainability. Leaders play a crucial role in fostering an environment where innovation and creativity can thrive. The Golden Rule—treating others as you would like to be treated—serves as a guiding principle for leaders to inspire and nurture these qualities within their teams. This chapter explores the importance of innovation and creativity, provides strategies for leaders to cultivate these attributes, and presents real-world examples to illustrate their impact on organizational culture and success.

Understanding Innovation and Creativity in the Workplace

Innovation involves the implementation of new ideas, processes, or products to improve organizational performance and create value. Creativity is the ability to generate novel and useful ideas. Both are critical for driving growth, solving problems, and maintaining a competitive edge.

The Importance of Innovation and Creativity

1. **Competitive Advantage**: Innovation and creativity help organizations differentiate themselves from competitors by offering unique products, services, and solutions (Porter, 1985).

2. **Adaptability and Resilience**: Organizations that foster innovation

and creativity are better equipped to adapt to changes and challenges in the market (Tushman & O'Reilly, 1996).

3. Employee Engagement and Satisfaction: A culture that encourages innovation and creativity enhances employee engagement, satisfaction, and retention (Amabile, 1997).

4. Growth and Profitability: Innovative organizations are more likely to achieve sustained growth and profitability through the continuous improvement of their offerings (Schumpeter, 1942).

The Role of the Golden Rule in Inspiring Innovation and Creativity

The Golden Rule provides a powerful framework for creating a supportive and inclusive environment where innovation and creativity can flourish. By treating others as you would like to be treated, leaders can foster trust, collaboration, and psychological safety, which are essential for innovative thinking.

Applying the Golden Rule to Foster Innovation and Creativity

1. Empathy and Understanding: Show empathy and understanding towards employees' ideas and perspectives. Create an environment where everyone feels heard and valued.

2. Respect and Recognition: Respect and recognize employees' creative contributions. Celebrate their successes and encourage them to pursue new ideas.

3. Support and Resources: Provide the necessary support and resources for employees to experiment and innovate. Remove barriers and provide the tools they need to succeed.

4. Trust and Psychological Safety: Build trust and psychological safety by encouraging risk-taking and learning from failures. Ensure that employees feel safe to share their ideas without fear of criticism or retribution.

Case Study: Google

Google's commitment to innovation and creativity is guided by the principles of the Golden Rule. The company's leaders foster an environment of empathy, respect, and support, where employees are encouraged to experiment and take risks. Google's open communication culture and emphasis on psychological safety have resulted in groundbreaking innovations such as Google Search, Google Maps, and Google Assistant (Schmidt & Rosenberg, 2014).

Strategies for Cultivating Innovation and Creativity

Cultivating innovation and creativity requires intentional efforts from leaders to create a supportive and stimulating work environment. The following strategies can help leaders inspire and nurture these qualities within their teams:

1. Encourage Open Communication and Collaboration

Open communication and collaboration are essential for generating and developing new ideas. Leaders should create opportunities for employees to share their thoughts and work together on innovative projects.

- **Foster Open Dialogue**: Hold regular brainstorming sessions, team meetings, and idea-sharing forums where employees can discuss new ideas and collaborate on projects.

- **Promote Cross-Functional Teams**: Encourage collaboration across different departments and functions to bring diverse perspectives and expertise to the table.

- **Use Collaborative Tools**: Implement collaborative tools and platforms that facilitate communication and idea-sharing, such as intranet forums, project management software, and virtual collaboration spaces.

Case Study: Pixar Animation Studios

Pixar Animation Studios is known for its collaborative culture, where open communication and teamwork are key to its creative success. The company's leadership encourages cross-functional collaboration and regular brainstorming sessions, fostering an environment where innovative ideas can flourish. This approach has resulted in numerous critically acclaimed and commercially successful films, including Toy Story, Finding Nemo, and Inside Out (Catmull & Wallace, 2014).

2. Provide Autonomy and Empowerment

Empowering employees with autonomy and decision-making authority fosters a sense of ownership and encourages creative problem-solving.

- **Delegate Responsibility**: Give employees the autonomy to make decisions and take ownership of their projects. Trust them to manage their work and contribute to the organization's goals.

- **Encourage Experimentation**: Encourage employees to experiment with new ideas and approaches. Support their efforts to innovate and learn from both successes and failures.

- **Recognize Initiative**: Recognize and reward employees who take initiative and demonstrate creativity. Highlight their contributions and set them as examples for others.

Case Study: 3M

3M's commitment to innovation is exemplified by its "15% Rule," which allows employees to spend 15% of their time working on projects of their own choosing. This autonomy has led to numerous innovative products, including Post-it Notes and Scotch Tape. By empowering employees to experiment and pursue their ideas, 3M has maintained its reputation as a leader in innovation (Gundling, 2000).

3. Foster a Culture of Continuous Learning

Continuous learning and development are essential for fostering innovation and creativity. Leaders should create opportunities for employees to acquire new knowledge and skills.

- **Provide Training and Development**: Offer training programs, workshops, and seminars that focus on creativity, innovation, and problem-solving skills. Encourage employees to participate in professional development opportunities.

- **Encourage Curiosity and Exploration**: Promote a culture of curiosity and exploration. Encourage employees to seek out new experiences, knowledge, and perspectives.

- **Support Learning from Failures**: Create an environment where failures are seen as learning opportunities. Encourage employees to reflect on and learn from their mistakes.

Case Study: IDEO

IDEO, a global design and innovation consultancy, fosters a culture of continuous learning by encouraging curiosity and exploration. The company's leadership supports employees' professional development and provides opportunities for learning and experimentation. This commitment to continuous learning has enabled IDEO to develop innovative solutions for a wide range of clients and industries (Kelley & Kelley, 2013).

4. Recognize and Reward Innovation

Recognition and rewards are powerful motivators for fostering innovation and creativity. Leaders should acknowledge and celebrate employees' creative contributions and achievements.

- **Implement Recognition Programs**: Develop recognition programs that highlight and reward innovative ideas and solutions. This can include awards, bonuses, and public acknowledgment.

- **Celebrate Milestones and Successes**: Celebrate key milestones and successes in the innovation process. Hold events, ceremonies, and celebrations to recognize employees' contributions.

- **Provide Incentives for Innovation**: Offer incentives for employees to pursue innovative projects. This can include funding for research and development, time off for creative pursuits, and opportunities for career advancement.

Case Study: Apple

Apple's commitment to innovation is reflected in its recognition and reward programs. The company's leadership recognizes and celebrates employees' creative contributions through awards, bonuses, and public acknowledgment. This approach has fostered a culture of innovation that has resulted in iconic products such as the iPhone, iPad, and MacBook (Isaacson, 2011).

The Impact of Innovation and Creativity on Organizational Success

The following real-world examples illustrate the impact of innovation and creativity on organizational success:

Case Study: Google

Google's commitment to innovation and creativity has driven its success as a global technology leader. The company's open communication culture, emphasis on psychological safety, and support for experimentation have resulted in groundbreaking innovations such as Google Search, Google Maps, and Google Assistant. By fostering an environment of empathy, respect, and support, Google has maintained its position at the forefront of technological innovation (Schmidt & Rosenberg, 2014).

Case Study: Pixar Animation Studios

Pixar Animation Studios' collaborative culture and emphasis on teamwork have resulted in numerous critically acclaimed and commercially successful films. The company's leadership encourages cross-functional collaboration and regular brainstorming sessions, fostering an environment where innovative ideas can flourish. This approach has made Pixar a leader in the animation industry (Catmull & Wallace, 2014).

Case Study: 3M

3M's "15% Rule" has enabled employees to spend a portion of their time working on projects of their own choosing, leading to numerous innovative products such as Post-it Notes and Scotch Tape. By empowering employees to experiment and pursue their ideas, 3M has maintained its reputation as a leader in innovation (Gundling, 2000).

Case Study: IDEO

IDEO's culture of continuous learning and exploration has enabled the company to develop innovative solutions for a wide range of clients and industries. The company's leadership supports employees' professional development and provides opportunities for learning and experimentation, fostering a culture of innovation (Kelley & Kelley, 2013).

Case Study: Apple

Apple's recognition and reward programs for innovative contributions have fostered a culture of creativity and excellence. The company's leadership recognizes and celebrates employees' creative contributions through awards, bonuses, and public acknowledgment. This approach has resulted in iconic products such as the iPhone, iPad, and MacBook, solidifying Apple's position as a leader in innovation (Isaacson, 2011).

Conclusion

Innovation and creativity are essential for organizational success and sustainability. By applying the Golden Rule—treating others as you would like to be treated—leaders can create a supportive and inclusive environment where these qualities can flourish. The principles of empathy, respect, support, and psychological safety provide a foundation for fostering innovation and creativity.

The strategies for cultivating innovation and creativity, such as encouraging open communication and collaboration, providing autonomy and empowerment, fostering a culture of continuous learning, and recognizing and rewarding innovation, help leaders inspire and nurture these qualities within their teams.

The impact of innovation and creativity on organizational success is evident in the real-world examples of Google, Pixar Animation Studios, 3M, IDEO, and Apple. These organizations have demonstrated that fostering a culture of innovation and creativity drives growth, adaptability, employee engagement, and profitability.

As we continue to explore the profound implications of ethical leadership and the Golden Rule in various leadership contexts, we aim to provide deeper insights into how these principles influence leadership behaviors, shape organizational cultures, and optimize operational effectiveness across diverse cultural landscapes. Through this exploration, we hope to inspire leaders to foster innovation and creativity, driving sustainable success and positive organizational climates.

References

Amabile, T. M. (1997). Motivating creativity in organizations: On doing what you love and loving what you do. *California Management Review, 40*(1), 39-58.

Catmull, E., & Wallace, A. (2014). *Creativity, Inc.: Overcoming the unseen forces that stand in the way of true inspiration*. Random House.

Gundling, E. (2000). *The 3M way to innovation: Balancing people and profit*. Kodansha International.

Isaacson, W. (2011). *Steve Jobs*. Simon & Schuster.

Kelley, T., & Kelley, D. (2013). *Creative confidence: Unleashing the creative potential within us all*. Crown Business.

Porter, M. E. (1985). *Competitive advantage: Creating and sustaining superior performance*. Free Press.

Schmidt, E., & Rosenberg, J. (2014). *How Google works*. Grand Central Publishing.

Schumpeter, J. A. (1942). *Capitalism, socialism, and democracy*. Harper & Brothers.

Tushman, M. L., & O'Reilly, C. A. (1996). Ambidextrous organizations: Managing evolutionary and revolutionary change. *California Management Review, 38*(4), 8-30.

Chapter 12

The Golden Rule in Crisis Leadership

Crisis situations present unique challenges for leaders, requiring swift, decisive, and ethical actions to navigate uncertainty and mitigate adverse impacts. The Golden Rule—treating others as you would like to be treated—offers a guiding principle for leaders to maintain integrity, build trust, and foster resilience during crises. This chapter explores the importance of ethical leadership in crisis situations, provides strategies for applying the Golden Rule, and presents real-world examples to illustrate its effectiveness.

Understanding Crisis Leadership

Crisis leadership involves guiding an organization through unexpected and disruptive events that threaten its stability and success. Effective crisis leadership requires clear communication, decisive action, empathy, and the ability to inspire and motivate teams under pressure.

Key Elements of Crisis Leadership

1. Decisiveness: The ability to make quick, informed decisions to address immediate threats and stabilize the situation (Boin, Hart, Stern, & Sundelius, 2005).

2. Communication: Clear, transparent, and timely communication to keep stakeholders informed and engaged (Coombs, 2007).

3. Empathy: Understanding and addressing the concerns and emotions of those affected by the crisis (Goleman et al., 2020).

4. Resilience: The capacity to recover and adapt to changing circumstances, maintaining focus on long-term goals (Mallak, 1998).

The Role of the Golden Rule in Crisis Leadership

The Golden Rule provides a moral compass for leaders navigating crises. By treating others as they would like to be treated, leaders can build trust, demonstrate empathy, and foster a sense of solidarity and resilience.

Applying the Golden Rule in Crisis Situations

1. Empathetic Communication: Communicate with empathy and understanding, addressing the concerns and emotions of stakeholders.

2. Transparent Decision-Making: Make decisions transparently, keeping stakeholders informed and involved in the process.

3. Support and Compassion: Provide support and compassion to those affected by the crisis, recognizing their struggles and offering assistance.

4. Fairness and Integrity: Ensure that actions and decisions are fair and just and uphold the organization's values and ethical standards.

Case Study: Johnson & Johnson's Tylenol Crisis

Johnson & Johnson's handling of the Tylenol crisis in 1982 is a prime example of applying the Golden Rule in crisis leadership. When cyanide-laced Tylenol capsules resulted in several deaths, the company faced a significant ethical dilemma. Johnson & Johnson's leaders prioritized customer safety and transparency, recalling all Tylenol products and communicating openly with the public. This empathetic and transparent approach helped the company rebuild trust and maintain its reputation for integrity (Brenner, 2009).

Strategies for Effective Crisis Leadership

Effective crisis leadership requires a strategic approach that integrates the principles of the Golden Rule. The following strategies can help leaders navigate crises ethically and effectively:

1. Establish a Crisis Management Plan

A well-prepared crisis management plan provides a framework for responding to crises swiftly and effectively.

- **Identify Potential Risks**: Conduct a risk assessment to identify potential crises that could impact the organization. Develop contingency plans for different scenarios.

- **Develop Response Protocols**: Establish clear protocols for responding to crises, including communication strategies, decision-making processes, and roles and responsibilities.

- **Train and Prepare**: Provide regular training and simulations to prepare leaders and employees for crisis situations. Ensure that everyone understands their roles and responsibilities.

Case Study: Toyota's Response to the 2010 Recall Crisis

In 2010, Toyota faced a significant crisis when reports of unintended acceleration led to a massive recall. The company's crisis management plan included clear response protocols and a commitment to transparency. Toyota's leaders communicated openly with customers and regulators, taking responsibility for the issue and implementing corrective measures. This proactive and transparent approach helped Toyota regain trust and maintain its reputation for quality (King & Baatartogtokh, 2015).

2. Communicate Transparently and Empathetically

Transparent and empathetic communication is crucial for maintaining trust and managing stakeholder expectations during a crisis.

- **Provide Regular Updates**: Communicate regularly with stakeholders, providing updates on the situation and the actions being taken to address it.

- **Listen and Respond**: Actively listen to stakeholders' concerns and respond empathetically. Address their questions and provide reassurance.

- **Be Honest and Transparent**: Be honest about the challenges and uncertainties faced. Avoid downplaying the severity of the crisis or withholding critical information.

Case Study: Southwest Airlines' Response to COVID-19

During the COVID-19 pandemic, Southwest Airlines maintained transparent and empathetic communication with its employees and customers. The company provided regular updates on safety measures, flight changes, and financial impacts. Southwest's leaders listened to employees' concerns and offered support, including job security assurances and health benefits. This transparent and empathetic approach helped maintain trust and loyalty during a challenging time (Parker, 2020).

3. Demonstrate Decisive and Ethical Leadership

Decisive and ethical leadership is essential for navigating crises effectively and maintaining stakeholder confidence.

- **Make Informed Decisions**: Gather relevant information and consult with experts to make informed decisions. Prioritize actions that protect stakeholders and uphold ethical standards.

- **Act Swiftly and Decisively**: Take swift and decisive action to address the crisis and mitigate its impact. Avoid delays that could exacerbate the situation.

- **Uphold Ethical Standards**: Ensure that all actions and decisions align with the organization's values and ethical standards. Avoid compromising ethics for short-term gains.

Case Study: Starbucks' Response to the Philadelphia Incident

In 2018, Starbucks faced a crisis when two African American men were arrested at a Philadelphia store, leading to accusations of racial bias. Starbucks' leadership responded swiftly and decisively, closing all U.S. stores for a day of racial bias training for employees. The company's leaders communicated openly about the incident, took responsibility, and implemented measures to prevent future occurrences. This decisive and ethical response helped Starbucks address the crisis and reinforce its commitment to diversity and inclusion (Schultz, 2018).

4. Foster a Culture of Resilience and Adaptability

A culture of resilience and adaptability helps organizations navigate crises and emerge stronger.

- **Encourage Flexibility**: Encourage employees to be flexible and adaptable in their roles and responsibilities. Provide opportunities for cross-training and skill development.

- **Support Mental Health and Well-Being**: Recognize the emotional impact of crises on employees and provide support for mental health and well-being. Offer resources such as counseling services and stress management programs.

- **Learn and Improve**: Use the crisis as a learning opportunity to identify areas for improvement. Conduct post-crisis reviews to evaluate the response and implement changes to enhance resilience.

Case Study: Airbnb's Response to the COVID-19 Pandemic

During the COVID-19 pandemic, Airbnb faced significant challenges as travel came to a halt. The company's leadership fostered a culture of resilience and adaptability, implementing measures to support hosts and guests, including flexible cancellation policies and health safety protocols. Airbnb also provides mental health resources and support for employees. This resilient and adaptable approach helped Airbnb navigate the crisis and position itself for recovery (Chesky, 2020).

Real-World Applications and Benefits

The following real-world examples illustrate the impact of applying the Golden Rule in crisis leadership:

Case Study: Johnson & Johnson's Tylenol Crisis

Johnson & Johnson's empathetic and transparent response to the Tylenol crisis helped rebuild trust and maintain its reputation for integrity. By prioritizing customer safety and communicating openly, the company demonstrated ethical leadership that resonated with stakeholders (Brenner, 2009).

Case Study: Toyota's Response to the 2010 Recall Crisis

Toyota's proactive and transparent response to the recall crisis helped the company regain trust and maintain its reputation for quality. By acting swiftly and communicating openly, Toyota demonstrated ethical leadership and a commitment to customer safety (King & Baatartogtokh, 2015).

Case Study: Southwest Airlines' Response to COVID-19

Southwest Airlines' transparent and empathetic communication during the COVID-19 pandemic helped maintain trust and loyalty among employees and customers. By listening to concerns and providing support, Southwest demonstrated ethical leadership that fostered resilience (Parker,

2020).

Case Study: Starbucks' Response to the Philadelphia Incident

Starbucks' decisive and ethical response to the Philadelphia incident reinforced the company's commitment to diversity and inclusion. By taking responsibility and implementing measures to prevent future occurrences, Starbucks demonstrated ethical leadership that resonated with stakeholders (Schultz, 2018).

Case Study: Airbnb's Response to the COVID-19 Pandemic

Airbnb's resilient and adaptable response to the COVID-19 pandemic helped the company navigate the crisis and position itself for recovery. By supporting hosts and guests and providing mental health resources for employees, Airbnb demonstrated ethical leadership that fostered resilience (Chesky, 2020).

Conclusion

Crisis leadership requires swift, decisive, and ethical actions to navigate uncertainty and mitigate adverse impacts. By applying the Golden Rule—treating others as you would like to be treated—leaders can build trust, demonstrate empathy, and foster resilience during crises.

The principles of empathetic communication, transparent decision-making, support and compassion, and fairness and integrity provide a framework for ethical crisis leadership. The strategies for effective crisis leadership, such as establishing a crisis management plan, communicating transparently and empathetically, demonstrating decisive and ethical leadership, and fostering a culture of resilience and adaptability, help leaders navigate crises ethically and effectively.

The real-world examples of Johnson & Johnson, Toyota, Southwest Airlines, Starbucks, and Airbnb illustrate the impact of applying the Golden Rule in crisis leadership. These organizations have demonstrated that ethical leadership drives trust, resilience, and long-term success.

As we conclude this book, we hope to have provided deeper insights into the role of ethical leadership and the Golden Rule in fostering sustainable success and positive organizational climates. By integrating these principles into their leadership practices, leaders can drive organizational success, create a positive impact on their teams and communities, and leave a lasting legacy of ethical leadership.

References

Boin, A., Hart, P., Stern, E., & Sundelius, B. (2005). *The politics of crisis management: Public leadership under pressure.* Cambridge University Press.

Brenner, S. N. (2009). Johnson & Johnson's Credo: A corporate cultural relic or a practical guide to employees. *Journal of Business Ethics, 85*(3), 219-223.

Chesky, B. (2020). Airbnb's response to COVID-19. Retrieved from https://news.airbnb.com/airbnbs-response-to-covid-19/

Coombs, W. T. (2007). *Ongoing crisis communication: Planning, managing, and responding.* Sage Publications.

Goleman, D., & Lenz, M. (2020). *Emotionally intelligent leader Daniel Goleman.* Findaway World.

King, A. A., & Baatartogtokh, B. (2015). How useful is the theory of disruptive innovation? *MIT Sloan Management Review, 57*(1), 77-90.

Mallak, L. A. (1998). Putting organizational resilience to work. *Industrial Management, 40*(6), 8-13.

Parker, A. (2020). Southwest Airlines' response to COVID-19. Retrieved from https://www.southwestaircommunity.com/t5/Blog/Southwest-s-Response-to-COVID-19/bc-p/105108

Schmidt, E., & Rosenberg, J. (2014). *How Google works.* Grand Central Publishing.

Schultz, H. (2018). *From the ground up: A journey to reimagine the promise of America.* Penguin Random House.

Chapter 13

The Golden Rule in Cross-Cultural Leadership

In an increasingly globalized world, leaders must navigate diverse cultural landscapes to effectively manage and inspire their teams. Cross-cultural leadership involves understanding and respecting cultural differences while fostering a cohesive and inclusive work environment. The Golden Rule—treating others as you would like to be treated—serves as a guiding principle for leaders to bridge cultural divides, build trust, and promote collaboration. This chapter explores the importance of cross-cultural leadership, provides strategies for applying the Golden Rule, and presents real-world examples to illustrate its impact on organizational success.

Understanding Cross-Cultural Leadership

Cross-cultural leadership involves leading and managing teams that comprise individuals from diverse cultural backgrounds. Effective cross-cultural leaders recognize and appreciate cultural differences, adapt their leadership styles, and create an inclusive environment where all team members feel valued and respected.

Key Elements of Cross-Cultural Leadership

1. **Cultural Awareness**: Understanding and appreciating cultural differences and their impact on communication, behavior, and work styles (Hofstede, 1991).

2. **Adaptability**: The ability to adapt leadership styles and approaches to suit different cultural contexts (Earley & Ang, 2003).

3. **Empathy**: Demonstrating empathy and understanding towards

team members from diverse cultural backgrounds (Stein, 2023).

4. Inclusion: Creating an inclusive environment that values and leverages cultural diversity (Shore et al., 2011).

The Role of the Golden Rule in Cross-Cultural Leadership

The Golden Rule provides a universal ethical framework that transcends cultural boundaries. By treating others as they would like to be treated, leaders can foster mutual respect, build trust, and promote collaboration across diverse cultural settings.

Applying the Golden Rule in Cross-Cultural Leadership

1. Empathy and Understanding: Show empathy and understanding towards team members' cultural backgrounds and perspectives. Take the time to learn about their cultures and traditions.

2. Respect and Inclusion: Respect cultural differences and create an inclusive environment where all team members feel valued and respected.

3. Open Communication: Foster open and transparent communication, ensuring that all team members feel comfortable expressing their ideas and concerns.

4. Fairness and Equity: Ensure that actions and decisions are fair and equitable, considering the diverse needs and perspectives of team members.

Case Study: Google's Cross-Cultural Leadership

Google's commitment to diversity and inclusion is guided by the principles of the Golden Rule. The company's leaders foster an inclusive environment where cultural differences are valued and leveraged. Google provides cultural competency training and encourages open communication, allowing team members from diverse backgrounds to collaborate effectively. This inclusive approach has contributed to Google's success as a global technology leader (Schmidt & Rosenberg, 2014).

Strategies for Effective Cross-Cultural Leadership

Effective cross-cultural leadership requires intentional efforts to understand and respect cultural differences while fostering an inclusive and collaborative environment. The following strategies can help leaders apply the Golden Rule in cross-cultural settings:

1. Develop Cultural Awareness

Cultural awareness is the foundation of cross-cultural leadership. Leaders should strive to understand and appreciate the cultural backgrounds of their team members.

- **Educate Yourself**: Learn about the cultural backgrounds of your team members. This includes understanding cultural norms, values, communication styles, and work behaviors.

- **Seek Cultural Competency Training**: Participate in cultural competency training programs to enhance your understanding of cultural differences and develop skills for effective cross-cultural communication.

- **Encourage Cultural Exchange**: Create opportunities for team members to share their cultural backgrounds and experiences. This can include cultural celebrations, workshops, and discussion forums.

Case Study: IBM's Global Leadership

IBM emphasizes cultural awareness in its global leadership practices. The company provides cultural competency training for leaders and encourages cultural exchange among employees. IBM's leaders actively seek to understand and respect cultural differences, fostering an inclusive and collaborative work environment. This commitment to cultural awareness has enabled IBM to effectively manage and inspire a diverse global workforce (Rometty, 2019).

2. Adapt Leadership Styles

Adaptability is crucial for effective cross-cultural leadership. Leaders should be flexible and adjust their leadership styles to suit different cultural contexts.

- **Understand Cultural Preferences**: Recognize that different cultures may have different preferences for leadership styles. For example, some cultures may value a more hierarchical approach, while others may prefer a more participative style.

- **Be Flexible**: Be willing to adjust your leadership style to accommodate the cultural preferences and needs of your team members. This may involve adopting different communication styles, decision-making processes, and motivational techniques.

- **Seek Feedback**: Regularly seek feedback from your team members on your leadership approach. Use this feedback to make adjustments and improve your effectiveness as a cross-cultural leader.

Case Study: Coca-Cola's Cross-Cultural Leadership

Coca-Cola's leaders demonstrate adaptability by adjusting their leadership styles to suit different cultural contexts. The company provides training and resources to help leaders understand and navigate cultural differences. By being flexible and responsive to the cultural preferences of their team members, Coca-Cola's leaders foster a cohesive and inclusive work environment across its global operations (Goizueta, 1997).

3. Foster Open and Transparent Communication

Open and transparent communication is essential for building trust and promoting collaboration in cross-cultural settings.

- **Encourage Open Dialogue**: Create an environment where team members feel comfortable expressing their ideas, concerns, and perspectives. Encourage open and honest communication.

- **Use Clear and Inclusive Language**: Use clear and inclusive language that is easily understood by all team members. Avoid jargon, idioms, and colloquialisms that may be confusing or exclusionary.

- **Provide Translation and Interpretation Services**: If needed, provide translation and interpretation services to ensure that all team members can participate fully in discussions and decision-making processes.

Case Study: Unilever's Inclusive Communication

Unilever prioritizes open and transparent communication in its cross-cultural leadership practices. The company encourages open dialogue and provides translation services to ensure that all team members can communicate effectively. Unilever's leaders use clear and inclusive language, fostering a collaborative and inclusive work environment. This commitment to open communication has contributed to Unilever's success as a global consumer goods company (Polman, 2016).

4. Create an Inclusive Environment

Creating an inclusive environment involves valuing and leveraging cultural diversity to promote collaboration and innovation.

- **Celebrate Cultural Diversity**: Recognize and celebrate the cultural diversity of your team. This can include cultural events, diversity awards, and recognition of cultural holidays.

- **Promote Equity and Inclusion**: Ensure that all team members have equal access to opportunities and resources. Implement policies and practices that promote equity and inclusion.

- **Leverage Diverse Perspectives**: Encourage team members to share their unique perspectives and experiences. Use these diverse insights to inform decision-making and drive innovation.

Case Study: Microsoft's Commitment to Inclusion

Microsoft's commitment to inclusion is evident in its cross-cultural leadership practices. The company celebrates cultural diversity through events, awards, and recognition of cultural holidays. Microsoft's leaders promote equity and inclusion, ensuring that all team members have equal access to opportunities and resources. By leveraging diverse perspectives, Microsoft fosters a culture of innovation and collaboration that drives its success (Nadella, 2017).

Real-World Applications and Benefits

The following real-world examples illustrate the impact of applying the Golden Rule in cross-cultural leadership:

Case Study: Google's Cross-Cultural Leadership

Google's inclusive approach to cross-cultural leadership has contributed to its success as a global technology leader. By valuing cultural differences, providing cultural competency training, and encouraging open communication, Google fosters a collaborative and innovative work environment (Schmidt & Rosenberg, 2014).

Case Study: IBM's Global Leadership

IBM's commitment to cultural awareness and inclusion has enabled it to effectively manage and inspire a diverse global workforce. By providing cultural competency training and encouraging cultural exchange, IBM's leaders foster an inclusive and collaborative work environment (Rometty, 2019).

Case Study: Coca-Cola's Cross-Cultural Leadership

Coca-Cola's adaptable leadership approach allows it to effectively navigate cultural differences and foster a cohesive and inclusive work environment across its global operations. By adjusting their leadership styles and seeking feedback, Coca-Cola's leaders promote collaboration and trust (Goizueta, 1997).

Case Study: Unilever's Inclusive Communication

Unilever's commitment to open and transparent communication fosters a collaborative and inclusive work environment. By encouraging open dialogue and providing translation services, Unilever's leaders ensure that all team members can communicate effectively and contribute to the organization's success (Polman, 2016).

Case Study: Microsoft's Commitment to Inclusion

Microsoft's inclusive leadership practices promote equity and leverage diverse perspectives to drive innovation and collaboration. By celebrating cultural diversity and promoting inclusion, Microsoft fosters a culture of trust and mutual respect that contributes to its success (Nadella, 2017).

Conclusion

Cross-cultural leadership is essential for effectively managing and inspiring diverse teams in a globalized world. By applying the Golden Rule—treating others as you would like to be treated—leaders can bridge cultural divides, build trust, and promote collaboration.

The principles of empathy, respect, open communication, and fairness provide a framework for effective cross-cultural leadership. The strategies for developing cultural awareness, adapting leadership styles, fostering open communication, and creating an inclusive environment help leaders apply the Golden Rule in cross-cultural settings.

The real-world examples of Google, IBM, Coca-Cola, Unilever, and Microsoft illustrate the impact of applying the Golden Rule in cross-cultural leadership. These organizations have demonstrated that fostering an inclusive and collaborative environment drives innovation, trust, and long-term success.

As we continue to explore the profound implications of ethical leadership and the Golden Rule in various leadership contexts, we hope to inspire leaders to embrace cross-cultural leadership and create positive organizational climates that leverage the strengths of diverse teams.

References

Earley, P. C., & Ang, S. (2003). *Cultural intelligence: Individual interactions across cultures*. Stanford University Press.

Stein, S. (2023). *Emotional intelligence*. Wiley Publishing, Inc.

Goizueta, R. (1997). *The leadership challenge: Coca-Cola's strategies for success*. Harvard Business Review Press.

Hofstede, G. (1991). *Cultures and organizations: Software of the mind*. McGraw-Hill.

Nadella, S. (2017). *Hit refresh: The quest to rediscover Microsoft's soul and imagine a better future for everyone*. Harper Business.

Polman, P. (2016). *Unilever's approach to inclusive leadership*. Retrieved from https://www.unilever.com/news/news-search/2016/unilevers-approach-to-inclusive-leadership.html

Rometty, G. (2019). *Good power: Leading positive change in our lives, work, and world*. Harvard Business Review Press.

Schmidt, E., & Rosenberg, J. (2014). *How Google works*. Grand Central Publishing.

Shore, L. M., Randel, A. E., Chung, B. G., Dean, M. A., Ehrhart, K. H., & Singh, G. (2011). Inclusion and diversity in work groups: A review and model for future research. *Journal of Management, 37*(4), 1262-1289.

Chapter 14

Future Challenges and Opportunities for Ethical Leadership

The future of leadership will be marked by unprecedented challenges and opportunities. In a world characterized by rapid technological advancements, increasing globalization, and shifting societal expectations, ethical leadership will be more critical than ever. This chapter explores the future challenges and opportunities for ethical leadership, providing insights into how leaders can navigate these complexities while upholding the principles of the Golden Rule.

Technological Advancements and Ethical Considerations

Technological advancements, particularly in artificial intelligence (AI), automation, and data analytics, are transforming industries and reshaping the workplace. These developments present both opportunities and ethical dilemmas for leaders.

Opportunities

1. Innovation and Efficiency: Technology can drive innovation and improve efficiency. AI and automation can streamline processes, reduce costs, and enhance productivity (Brynjolfsson & McAfee, 2014).

2. Data-Driven Decision-Making: Advanced analytics enable leaders to make more informed decisions by providing deeper insights into market trends, customer behavior, and operational performance (Mayer-Schönberger & Cukier, 2013).

3. Enhanced Connectivity: Digital tools facilitate better communication and collaboration across geographically dispersed teams, fostering a more connected and inclusive workplace (Gartner, 2019).

Challenges

1. Privacy and Security: The increasing use of data raises concerns about privacy and security. Leaders must ensure that data is handled responsibly and that privacy is protected (Zuboff, 2019).

2. Bias and Fairness: AI algorithms can perpetuate biases if not designed and monitored carefully. Leaders must address these biases to ensure fairness and equity in decision-making (O'Neil, 2016).

3. Job Displacement: Automation and AI may lead to job displacement, raising ethical questions about the future of work and the need for retraining and support for affected workers (Frey & Osborne, 2017).

Ethical Leadership Strategies

1. Transparent Communication: Clearly communicate the implications of technological changes to employees and stakeholders. Address concerns openly and provide reassurance about the organization's commitment to ethical practices.

2. Inclusive Decision Making: Involve diverse teams in the development and implementation of technological solutions to mitigate biases and ensure that different perspectives are considered.

3. Continuous Learning and Development: Invest in training and development programs to help employees adapt to new technologies. Provide support for those affected by job displacement.

Case Study: Microsoft's Ethical AI Initiative

Microsoft has taken a proactive approach to addressing the ethical implications of AI. The company established the AI and Ethics in Engineering and Research (AETHER) Committee to oversee the responsible development and deployment of AI technologies. Microsoft's commitment to transparency, inclusivity, and continuous learning exemplifies ethical leadership in the face of technological advancements (Nadella, 2017).

Globalization and Cross-Cultural Leadership

Globalization has created a more interconnected world, bringing diverse cultures and markets together. This interconnectedness presents both opportunities and challenges for leaders.

Opportunities

1. Diverse Perspectives: Globalization brings diverse perspectives and ideas, fostering innovation and creativity. Leaders can leverage this diversity to drive organizational success (Hofstede, 1991).

2. Market Expansion: Global markets offer opportunities for expansion and growth. Leaders can tap into new customer bases and explore international partnerships (Friedman, 2005).

3. Talent Pool: Access to a global talent pool allows organizations to attract and retain top talent from around the world, enhancing their competitive advantage (Tung, 2008).

Challenges

1. Cultural Differences: Navigating cultural differences can be challenging. Misunderstandings and miscommunications can arise, leading to conflicts and inefficiencies (Earley & Ang, 2003).

2. Ethical Standards: Different countries have varying ethical standards and regulations. Leaders must ensure that their organizations adhere to consistent ethical practices across all locations (Donaldson, 1996).

3. Geopolitical Risks: Global operations expose organizations to geopolitical risks, including political instability, trade conflicts, and regulatory changes (Kobrin, 2017).

Ethical Leadership Strategies

1. Cultural Competence: Develop cultural competence by understanding and respecting different cultural norms and values. Provide cultural competency training for employees and leaders.

2. Global Ethical Standards: Establish global ethical standards that align with the organization's values. Ensure that these standards are upheld consistently across all locations.

3. **Risk Management**: Implement robust risk management strategies to navigate geopolitical risks. Stay informed about global developments and be prepared to adapt to changes.

Case Study: Unilever's Sustainable Living Plan

Unilever's Sustainable Living Plan demonstrates the company's commitment to ethical leadership on a global scale. The plan focuses on improving health and well-being, reducing environmental impact, and enhancing livelihoods. Unilever's efforts to uphold consistent ethical standards and promote sustainability across its global operations highlight the importance of ethical leadership in a globalized world (Polman, 2016).

Societal Shifts and Corporate Social Responsibility

Societal expectations regarding corporate responsibility are evolving. Stakeholders increasingly demand that organizations take meaningful action on social and environmental issues.

Opportunities

1. **Reputation and Trust**: Demonstrating a commitment to social responsibility enhances the organization's reputation and builds trust with stakeholders (Porter & Kramer, 2006).

2. **Employee Engagement**: Employees are more likely to be engaged and motivated when they work for organizations that align with their values and contribute to societal well-being (Bhattacharya, Sen, & Korschun, 2008).

3. **Sustainable Growth**: Addressing social and environmental issues can drive long-term sustainable growth by creating shared value for the organization and society (Porter & Kramer, 2011).

Challenges

1. **Balancing Priorities**: Balancing financial performance with social and environmental responsibilities can be challenging. Leaders must navigate trade-offs and prioritize actions that deliver the greatest impact (Freeman, Harrison, Wicks, Parmar, & de Colle, 2010).

2. **Measuring Impact**: Measuring the impact of social responsibility initiatives can be complex. Leaders must develop robust metrics and

frameworks to assess progress and outcomes (Epstein & Buhovac, 2014).

3. Stakeholder Expectations: Managing diverse stakeholder expectations requires effective communication and engagement. Leaders must ensure that their actions align with stakeholder values and concerns (Freeman, 1984).

Ethical Leadership Strategies

1. Integrate CSR into Strategy: Integrate corporate social responsibility (CSR) into the organization's strategic vision and operations. Ensure that CSR initiatives align with the organization's values and goals.

2. Engage Stakeholders: Actively engage stakeholders in the development and implementation of CSR initiatives. Seek input and feedback to ensure that actions align with stakeholder expectations.

3. Measure and Communicate Impact: Develop metrics and frameworks to measure the impact of CSR initiatives. Communicate progress and outcomes transparently to stakeholders.

Case Study: Patagonia's Environmental Initiatives

Patagonia is renowned for its commitment to environmental sustainability. The company integrates environmental responsibility into its business strategy, from sourcing materials to manufacturing processes. Patagonia's efforts to measure and communicate the impact of its initiatives demonstrate ethical leadership and a commitment to creating shared value (Chouinard & Stanley, 2022).

Resilience and Adaptability in Leadership

The ability to navigate uncertainty and adapt to change is critical for future leaders. Resilience and adaptability enable organizations to thrive in dynamic environments.

Opportunities

1. Innovation and Growth: Resilient and adaptable organizations are better positioned to innovate and capitalize on new opportunities. Leaders can foster a culture of continuous improvement and learning (Hamel & Välikangas, 2003).

2. **Employee Empowerment**: Empowering employees to adapt and respond to change enhances engagement and performance. Leaders can create an environment where employees feel supported and valued (Dweck, 2006).

3. **Sustainable Success**: Building resilience and adaptability contributes to long-term sustainable success. Organizations can navigate challenges and emerge stronger (Lengnick-Hall & Beck, 2005).

Challenges

1. **Uncertainty and Complexity**: Navigating uncertainty and complexity requires strong leadership and effective decision-making. Leaders must be prepared to manage ambiguity and change (Heifetz, Grashow, & Linsky, 2009).

2. **Resource Allocation**: Allocating resources effectively in dynamic environments can be challenging. Leaders must prioritize initiatives that drive resilience and adaptability (Sull, 2009).

3. **Cultural Resistance**: Organizational cultures that resist change can hinder adaptability. Leaders must foster a culture that embraces innovation and continuous improvement (Kotter, 1996).

Ethical Leadership Strategies

1. **Foster a Learning Culture**: Promote a culture of continuous learning and development. Encourage employees to seek new knowledge and skills and support their growth.

2. **Empower Employees**: Empower employees to take initiative and make decisions. Provide the resources and support they need to adapt and respond to change.

3. **Lead by Example**: Demonstrate resilience and adaptability in your own leadership. Model behaviors that promote a positive and proactive approach to change.

Case Study: Google's Approach to Innovation

Google's culture of innovation and continuous improvement exemplifies resilience and adaptability. The company encourages employees to pursue new ideas and take risks, fostering a dynamic and innovative environment. Google's commitment to learning and development supports its ability to navigate uncertainty and drive sustainable success (Schmidt & Rosenberg, 2014).

Conclusion

The future of ethical leadership will be shaped by the challenges and opportunities presented by technological advancements, globalization, societal shifts, and the need for resilience and adaptability. Leaders who embrace the principles of the Golden Rule—treating others as you would like to be treated—will be well-equipped to navigate these complexities and drive positive change.

By fostering ethical behavior, building trust, and promoting a culture of inclusivity and innovation, leaders can create organizations that are resilient, sustainable, and capable of thriving in a rapidly changing world. The lessons learned from the case studies and best practices explored in this chapter provide a roadmap for leaders to follow as they embrace the future with ethical leadership.

References

Bhattacharya, C. B., Sen, S., & Korschun, D. (2008). Using corporate social responsibility to win the war for talent. *MIT Sloan Management Review, 49*(2), 37-44.

Brynjolfsson, E., & McAfee, A. (2014). *The second machine age: Work, progress, and prosperity in a time of brilliant technologies.* W. W. Norton & Company.

Chouinard, Y., & Stanley, V. (2023). *The future of the responsible company: What we've learned from Patagonia's first 50 Years.* Patagonia.

Donaldson, T. (1996). Values in tension: Ethics away from home. *Harvard Business Review, 74*(5), 48-62.

Dweck, C. S. (2006). *Mindset: The new psychology of success.* Random House.

Earley, P. C., & Ang, S. (2003). *Cultural intelligence: Individual interactions across cultures.* Stanford University Press.

Epstein, M. J., & Buhovac, A. R. (2014). *Making sustainability work: Best practices in managing and measuring corporate social, environmental, and economic impacts*. Berrett-Koehler Publishers.

Freeman, R. E. (1984). *Strategic management: A stakeholder approach.* Pitman.

Freeman, R. E., Harrison, J. S., Wicks, A. C., Parmar, B. L., & de Colle, S. (2010). *Stakeholder theory: The state of the art.* Cambridge University Press.

Frey, C. B., & Osborne, M. A. (2017). The future of employment: How susceptible are jobs to computerisation? *Technological Forecasting and Social Change, 114,* 254-280.

Friedman, T. L. (2005). *The world is flat: A brief history of the twenty-first century.* Farrar, Straus and Giroux.

Gartner. (2019). Future of work trends: Enhancing productivity through digital tools. Retrieved from https://www.gartner.com/en/newsroom/press-releases/2019-06-03-gartner-identifies-three-future-of-work-trends

Hamel, G., & Välikangas, L. (2003). The quest for resilience. *Harvard Business Review, 81*(9), 52-63.

Heifetz, R., Grashow, A., & Linsky, M. (2009). *The practice of adaptive leadership: Tools and tactics for changing your organization and the world.* Harvard Business Press.

Hofstede, G. (1991). *Cultures and organizations: Software of the mind.* McGraw-Hill.

Kobrin, S. J. (2017). Globalization, transnational corporations, and the future of global governance. In A. Brysk (Ed.), *Globalization and human rights* (pp. 50-70). University of California Press.

Kotter, J. P. (1996). *Leading change.* Harvard Business School Press.

Lengnick-Hall, C. A., & Beck, T. E. (2005). Adaptive fit versus robust transformation: How organizations respond to environmental change. *Journal of Management, 31*(5), 738-757.

Mayer-Schönberger, V., & Cukier, K. (2013). *Big data: A revolution that will transform how we live, work, and think.* Houghton Mifflin Harcourt.

Nadella, S. (2017). *Hit refresh: The quest to rediscover Microsoft's soul and imagine a better future for everyone.* Harper Business.

O'Neil, C. (2016). *Weapons of math destruction: How big data increases inequality and threatens democracy.* Crown Publishing Group.

Polman, P. (2016). *Unilever's approach to inclusive leadership.* Retrieved from https://www.unilever.com/news/news-search/2016/unilevers-approach-to-inclusive-leadership.html

Porter, M. E., & Kramer, M. R. (2006). Strategy and society: The link between competitive advantage and corporate social responsibility. *Harvard Business Review, 84*(12), 78-92.

Porter, M. E., & Kramer, M. R. (2011). Creating shared value. *Harvard Business Review, 89*(1/2), 62-77.

Schmidt, E., & Rosenberg, J. (2014). *How Google works.* Grand Central Publishing.

Sull, D. (2009). How to thrive in turbulent markets. *Harvard Business Review, 87*(2), 78-88.

Tung, R. L. (2008). The cross-cultural research imperative: The need to balance cross-national and intra-national diversity. *Journal of International Business Studies, 39*(1), 41-46.

Zuboff, S. (2019). *The age of surveillance capitalism: The fight for a human future at the new frontier of power.* PublicAffairs.

Chapter 15

Building Ethical Leadership in Future Generations

As we look ahead to the future, the responsibility of nurturing ethical leadership falls on the current generation of leaders. Ensuring that future leaders are equipped with the principles of the Golden Rule—treating others as you would like to be treated—is essential for fostering a culture of integrity, empathy, and fairness. This chapter explores strategies for developing ethical leadership in future generations, providing insights into the role of education, mentorship, and organizational culture in this process.

The Importance of Ethical Leadership Development

Developing ethical leadership in future generations is crucial for several reasons. First, it ensures the continuity of ethical practices within organizations, leading to sustained success and positive social impact. Second, ethical leaders are better equipped to navigate the complexities of modern business environments, making decisions that are not only profitable but also socially responsible. Finally, fostering ethical leadership helps build a more just and equitable society.

Core Components of Ethical Leadership Development

1. **Education and Training**: Providing formal education and training on ethical principles and decision-making.

2. **Mentorship and Role Modeling**: Encouraging experienced leaders to mentor and serve as role models for emerging leaders.

3. **Organizational Culture**: Creating an organizational culture that

values and promotes ethical behavior.

Education and Training

Education is the foundation of ethical leadership development. By integrating ethics into the curriculum, educational institutions can play a vital role in shaping the values and principles of future leaders.

Formal Education

1. Ethics Courses: Incorporate ethics courses into business and leadership programs. These courses should cover fundamental ethical theories, principles, and frameworks, as well as practical applications in business contexts.

2. Case Studies: Use case studies to illustrate real-world ethical dilemmas and the impact of ethical and unethical decisions. Analyzing these cases helps students understand the complexities of ethical decision-making and develop critical thinking skills.

3. Interdisciplinary Approach: Encourage an interdisciplinary approach to ethics education, integrating insights from philosophy, sociology, psychology, and other fields. This broad perspective helps students appreciate the multifaceted nature of ethical issues.

Experiential Learning

1. Internships and Practicums: Provide opportunities for students to engage in internships and practicums where they can observe and practice ethical leadership in real-world settings. These experiences help bridge the gap between theoretical knowledge and practical application.

2. Simulations and Role-Playing: Use simulations and role-playing exercises to create realistic scenarios where students must navigate ethical dilemmas. These activities promote active learning and allow students to experiment with different approaches to ethical decision-making.

3. Service Learning: Incorporate service-learning projects that involve working with communities and addressing social issues. These projects foster empathy, social responsibility, and a commitment to ethical behavior.

Case Study: Harvard Business School

Harvard Business School integrates ethics into its MBA curriculum through courses, case studies, and experiential learning opportunities. The school emphasizes the importance of ethical leadership and encourages students to consider the broader social implications of business decisions. Harvard's approach to ethics education helps prepare future leaders to navigate complex ethical challenges with integrity (Harvard Business School, 2020).

Mentorship and Role Modeling

Mentorship and role modeling are critical components of ethical leadership development. Experienced leaders can provide guidance, support, and inspiration to emerging leaders, helping them internalize ethical principles and practices.

Mentorship Programs

1. Structured Mentorship: Implement structured mentorship programs that pair emerging leaders with experienced mentors. These programs should focus on developing ethical leadership skills and fostering a supportive relationship between mentors and mentees.

2. Mentor Training: Provide training for mentors to ensure they understand their role in promoting ethical leadership. Training should cover effective mentorship techniques, ethical principles, and strategies for addressing ethical dilemmas.

3. Regular Check-Ins: Establish regular check-ins between mentors and mentees to discuss progress, challenges, and ethical issues. These check-ins provide ongoing support and reinforce the importance of ethical behavior.

Role Modeling

1. Visible Ethical Behavior: Leaders should model ethical behavior in their actions and decisions. By demonstrating integrity, fairness, and empathy, leaders set a positive example for others to follow.

2. Open Communication: Encourage open communication about ethical issues within the organization. Leaders should share their experiences and insights on ethical decision-making, fostering a culture of transparency and learning.

3. Recognition of Ethical Behavior: Recognize and celebrate ethical behavior within the organization. Highlighting examples of ethical leadership reinforces the organization's values and encourages others to act ethically.

Case Study: Johnson & Johnson

Johnson & Johnson's Credo serves as a guiding framework for ethical behavior within the organization. The company's leaders model ethical behavior and actively engage in mentorship programs to develop future leaders. This commitment to mentorship and role modeling has helped Johnson & Johnson maintain a strong ethical culture and reputation (Brenner, 2009).

Organizational Culture

Creating an organizational culture that values and promotes ethical behavior is essential for developing ethical leadership. Organizational culture shapes the attitudes and behaviors of employees and influences their decision-making processes.

Values and Principles

1. Clear Ethical Standards: Establish clear ethical standards and principles that guide behavior within the organization. These standards should be communicated to all employees and integrated into the organization's policies and practices.

2. Mission and Vision Alignment: Ensure that the organization's mission and vision align with its ethical values. Leaders should articulate a clear vision that emphasizes the importance of ethical behavior and social responsibility.

3. Consistent Messaging: Consistently reinforce the organization's ethical values through messaging, communication, and actions. This consistency helps embed ethical principles into the organizational culture.

Policies and Practices

1. **Ethics Training**: Provide regular ethics training for all employees. Training should cover the organization's ethical standards, decision-making frameworks, and strategies for addressing ethical dilemmas.

2. **Ethics Committees**: Establish ethics committees to oversee ethical issues within the organization. These committees can provide guidance, review policies, and address ethical concerns.

3. **Reporting Mechanisms**: Implement mechanisms for reporting ethical concerns and violations. Ensure that employees feel safe and supported in reporting issues and that there are clear processes for addressing them.

Case Study: Patagonia

Patagonia's commitment to environmental sustainability and social responsibility is embedded in its organizational culture. The company emphasizes ethical behavior in its mission and values, provides ethics training for employees, and has established mechanisms for reporting ethical concerns. Patagonia's strong ethical culture has contributed to its reputation as a responsible and sustainable business (Chouinard & Stanley, 2022).

Developing Future Leaders through Continuous Learning

Continuous learning is essential for developing ethical leadership. The rapidly changing business environment requires leaders to stay informed and adaptable, continuously honing their skills and knowledge.

Professional Development

1. **Ongoing Education**: Encourage ongoing education and professional development for leaders at all levels. This can include attending conferences, enrolling in courses, and participating in workshops on ethics and leadership.

2. **Leadership Development Programs**: Implement leadership development programs that focus on ethical leadership. These programs should provide opportunities for leaders to learn from experts, engage in reflective practices, and develop their ethical decision-making skills.

3. Learning Communities: Create learning communities within the organization where leaders can share insights, experiences, and best practices related to ethical leadership. These communities foster a culture of continuous learning and support.

Reflective Practices

1. Self-Reflection: Encourage leaders to engage in self-reflection to assess their values, behaviors, and decisions. Reflective practices help leaders align their actions with their ethical principles and identify areas for improvement.

2. Feedback and Evaluation: Provide regular feedback and evaluation to leaders on their ethical behavior and decision-making. Constructive feedback helps leaders understand their strengths and areas for growth.

3. Ethical Journals: Suggest that leaders maintain ethical journals to document their experiences, reflections, and learnings related to ethical leadership. Journaling promotes self-awareness and continuous improvement.

Case Study: Google's Leadership Development Programs

Google invests heavily in leadership development programs that emphasize ethical leadership. The company provides ongoing education, leadership training, and reflective practices for its leaders. Google's commitment to continuous learning helps ensure that its leaders are equipped to navigate ethical challenges and foster a positive organizational culture (Schmidt & Rosenberg, 2014).

Conclusion

Building ethical leadership in future generations is a critical responsibility for current leaders. By prioritizing education and training, mentorship and role modeling, and fostering an organizational culture that values ethical behavior, leaders can ensure the continuity of ethical practices within their organizations. Continuous learning and development further support the growth of ethical leaders who are prepared to navigate the complexities of the modern business environment with integrity and compassion.

The principles of the Golden Rule—treating others as you would like to be treated—serve as a guiding framework for developing ethical leadership.

By embracing these principles, leaders can create a positive and lasting impact on their organizations and the broader community. As we look to the future, the commitment to ethical leadership will remain a cornerstone of sustainable success and social responsibility.

References

Brenner, S. N. (2009). Johnson & Johnson's Credo: A corporate cultural relic or a practical guide to employees. *Journal of Business Ethics, 85*(3), 219-223.

Chouinard, Y., & Stanley, V. (2023). *The future of the responsible company: What we've learned from Patagonia's first 50 Years.* Patagonia.

Harvard Business School. (2020). *MBA program.* Retrieved from https://www.hbs.edu/mba/

Nadella, S. (2017). *Hit refresh: The quest to rediscover Microsoft's soul and imagine a better future for everyone.* Harper Business.

Schmidt, E., & Rosenberg, J. (2014). *How Google works.* Grand Central Publishing.

Chapter 16

Measuring the Impact of Ethical Leadership

In an era where accountability and transparency are increasingly valued, it is essential for organizations to measure the impact of ethical leadership. Ethical leadership, guided by the Golden Rule—treating others as you would like to be treated—has profound implications for organizational culture, employee engagement, and overall performance. However, to ensure that these principles are effectively integrated and to demonstrate their value, leaders must develop robust methods for measuring their impact.

The Importance of Measuring Ethical Leadership

Measuring ethical leadership is critical for several reasons. First, it provides insights into how well ethical principles are being integrated into the organization's operations. Second, it helps identify areas for improvement and guides the development of strategies to enhance ethical behavior. Third, it demonstrates the value of ethical leadership to stakeholders, building trust and credibility. Finally, it ensures accountability, as leaders and employees are held responsible for maintaining ethical standards.

Core Components of Measuring Ethical Leadership

1. **Ethical Climate Surveys**: Assessing the perception of ethical behavior within the organization.

2. **Performance Metrics**: Linking ethical leadership to organizational performance indicators.

3. **Behavioral Assessments**: Evaluating the ethical behavior of leaders and employees.

4. **Stakeholder Feedback**: Gathering feedback from various stakeholders on the organization's ethical practices.

Ethical Climate Surveys

Ethical climate surveys are a valuable tool for assessing the perception of ethical behavior within an organization. These surveys help gauge the overall ethical climate, identify potential issues, and measure the effectiveness of ethical leadership initiatives.

Designing Ethical Climate Surveys

1. **Survey Content**: Include questions that assess the perception of ethical behavior, the effectiveness of ethical policies, and the overall ethical climate. Questions should cover areas such as trust, integrity, fairness, and respect.

2. **Anonymity and Confidentiality**: Ensure that responses are anonymous and confidential to encourage honest feedback. This helps in obtaining accurate and reliable data.

3. **Frequency**: Conduct ethical climate surveys regularly, such as annually or biannually, to track changes over time and assess the impact of initiatives.

Analyzing Survey Results

1. **Quantitative Analysis**: Analyze quantitative data to identify trends and patterns. Use statistical methods to compare results across different departments and time periods.

2. **Qualitative Analysis**: Analyze open-ended responses to gain deeper insights into specific issues and concerns. Identify recurring themes and areas for improvement.

3. **Actionable Insights**: Use survey results to develop actionable insights and strategies for enhancing the ethical climate. Communicate findings and action plans to employees and stakeholders.

Case Study: Google's Ethical Climate Surveys

Google conducts regular ethical climate surveys to assess the perception of ethical behavior within the organization. The surveys cover areas such as trust, fairness, and respect, providing valuable insights into the effectiveness of ethical leadership initiatives. Google uses the survey results to develop strategies for enhancing the ethical climate and addressing identified issues (Schmidt & Rosenberg, 2014).

Performance Metrics

Linking ethical leadership to organizational performance indicators helps demonstrate the value of ethical behavior. Performance metrics can provide a quantitative measure of the impact of ethical leadership on various aspects of organizational performance.

Key Performance Metrics

1. Employee Engagement: Measure employee engagement levels through surveys and feedback mechanisms. High levels of engagement are often linked to ethical leadership and a positive organizational culture (Peters, 2019).

2. Employee Retention: Track employee retention rates as an indicator of organizational health. Ethical leadership can contribute to higher retention rates by fostering a supportive and respectful work environment (Allen & Meyer, 1990).

3. Customer Satisfaction: Assess customer satisfaction levels through surveys and feedback. Ethical behavior and integrity can enhance customer trust and loyalty (Parasuraman, Zeithaml, & Berry, 1985).

4. Financial Performance: Analyze financial performance metrics, such as revenue growth, profitability, and return on investment (ROI). Ethical leadership can drive sustainable financial performance by building trust and reputation (Porter & Kramer, 2006).

Integrating Performance Metrics

1. Balanced Scorecard: Use a balanced scorecard approach to integrate ethical leadership metrics into overall performance measurement. This approach ensures that ethical behavior is aligned with organizational goals and objectives (Kaplan & Norton, 1996).

2. Benchmarking: Benchmark performance metrics against industry standards and best practices. This helps identify areas for improvement and set realistic targets.

3. Continuous Monitoring: Continuously monitor performance metrics to assess the ongoing impact of ethical leadership. Regularly review and update metrics to ensure they remain relevant and accurate.

Case Study: Johnson & Johnson's Credo Metrics

Johnson & Johnson uses a balanced scorecard approach to integrate ethical leadership metrics into its overall performance measurement. The company's Credo, which emphasizes ethical behavior and social responsibility, is linked to performance metrics such as employee engagement, customer satisfaction, and financial performance. This approach helps Johnson & Johnson demonstrate the value of ethical leadership and ensure accountability (Brenner, 2009).

Behavioral Assessments

Behavioral assessments evaluate the ethical behavior of leaders and employees, providing insights into how well ethical principles are being practiced within the organization.

Types of Behavioral Assessments

1. 360-Degree Feedback: Use 360-degree feedback assessments to gather feedback from peers, subordinates, and supervisors on an individual's ethical behavior. This comprehensive approach provides a well-rounded view of ethical conduct (Lepsinger & Lucia, 1997).

2. Self-Assessments: Encourage leaders and employees to conduct self-assessments of their ethical behavior. Self-reflection helps individuals identify areas for improvement and commit to ethical principles (Stein, 2023).

3. Ethical Behavior Audits: Conduct regular audits of ethical behavior within the organization. These audits can assess compliance with ethical standards, identify potential issues, and recommend corrective actions (Sims, 1992).

Implementing Behavioral Assessments

1. Clear Criteria: Establish clear criteria for assessing ethical behavior. Criteria should be based on the organization's values and ethical standards.

2. Training and Development: Provide training and development programs to help individuals improve their ethical behavior. Focus on building skills such as integrity, empathy, and ethical decision-making.

3. Feedback and Support: Provide constructive feedback and support to individuals based on assessment results. Encourage continuous improvement and recognize positive behavior.

Case Study: IBM's 360-Degree Feedback Program

IBM uses a 360-degree feedback program to assess the ethical behavior of its leaders and employees. The program gathers feedback from multiple sources, providing a comprehensive view of an individual's conduct. IBM uses the results to develop personalized training and development plans, helping individuals enhance their ethical behavior and align with the organization's values (Rometty, 2019).

Stakeholder Feedback

Gathering feedback from various stakeholders on the organization's ethical practices provides valuable insights into the external perception of ethical leadership.

Types of Stakeholder Feedback

1. Customer Feedback: Collect feedback from customers on their experiences with the organization. Customer feedback can provide insights into the impact of ethical behavior on customer trust and satisfaction (Parasuraman, Zeithaml, & Berry, 1985).

2. Supplier Feedback: Engage suppliers to gather feedback on the organization's ethical practices. Supplier feedback helps assess the impact of ethical leadership on business relationships and supply chain integrity (Porter & Kramer, 2006).

3. Community Feedback: Seek feedback from the community and other external stakeholders. Community feedback can provide insights into the organization's social responsibility and impact on society (Freeman, 1984).

Integrating Stakeholder Feedback

1. Regular Surveys: Conduct regular surveys to gather feedback from various stakeholders. Use standardized questions to ensure consistency and reliability.

2. Focus Groups: Organize focus groups with key stakeholders to discuss ethical practices and gather in-depth feedback. Focus groups provide qualitative insights that complement survey data.

3. Public Reporting: Transparently report on stakeholder feedback and the organization's ethical practices. Public reporting builds trust and demonstrates accountability.

Case Study: Patagonia's Stakeholder Engagement

Patagonia actively engages with its stakeholders to gather feedback on its ethical practices. The company conducts regular surveys and focus groups with customers, suppliers, and community members. Patagonia uses the feedback to improve its social responsibility initiatives and ensure alignment with stakeholder values (Chouinard & Stanley, 2022).

Conclusion

Measuring the impact of ethical leadership is essential for ensuring accountability, demonstrating value, and fostering continuous improvement. By utilizing ethical climate surveys, performance metrics, behavioral assessments, and stakeholder feedback, organizations can gain comprehensive insights into the effectiveness of their ethical leadership initiatives. Ethical leadership, guided by the Golden Rule, has a profound impact on organizational culture, employee engagement, and overall performance. By developing robust methods for measuring this impact, leaders can ensure that ethical principles are effectively integrated and continuously improved.

The case studies of Google, Johnson & Johnson, IBM, and Patagonia illustrate the practical application of these measurement strategies. These organizations demonstrate that by prioritizing ethical leadership and measuring its impact, they can build trust, enhance performance, and create a positive social impact. As organizations navigate the complexities of the modern business environment, the commitment to ethical leadership and the principles of the Golden Rule will remain essential for sustainable success and positive social responsibility.

References

Allen, N. J., & Meyer, J. P. (1990). The measurement and antecedents of affective, continuance and normative commitment to the organization. *Journal of Occupational Psychology, 63*(1), 1-18.

Brenner, S. N. (2009). Johnson & Johnson's Credo: A corporate cultural relic or a practical guide to employees. *Journal of Business Ethics, 85*(3), 219-223.

Chouinard, Y., & Stanley, V. (2023). *The future of the responsible company: What we've learned from Patagonia's first 50 Years.* Patagonia.

Freeman, R. E. (1984). *Strategic management: A stakeholder approach.* Pitman.

Kaplan, R. S., & Norton, D. P. (1996). *The balanced scorecard: Translating strategy into action.* Harvard Business School Press.

Lepsinger, R., & Lucia, A. D. (1997). *The art and science of 360-degree feedback.* Pfeiffer.

Parasuraman, A., Zeithaml, V. A., & Berry, L. L. (1985). A conceptual model of service quality and its implications for future research. *Journal of Marketing, 49*(4), 41-50.

Peters, J. (2019). *Employee engagement: Creating high positive energy at work.* Knowledge Resources.

Porter, M. E., & Kramer, M. R. (2006). Strategy and society: The link between competitive advantage and corporate social responsibility. *Harvard Business Review, 84*(12), 78-92.

Rometty, G. (2019). *Good power: Leading positive change in our lives, work, and world.* Harvard Business Review Press.

Schmidt, E., & Rosenberg, J. (2014). *How Google works.* Grand Central Publishing.

Sims, R. R. (1992). The challenge of ethical behavior in organizations. *Journal of Business Ethics, 11*(7), 505-513.

Stein, S. (2023). *Emotional intelligence.* Wiley Publishing, Inc.

Chapter 16

Resources for Further Reading and Professional Development

As we conclude this exploration of ethical leadership, it is essential to provide resources for further reading and professional development. Ethical leadership, guided by the Golden Rule—treating others as you would like to be treated—is a lifelong journey of learning, reflection, and growth. This chapter offers a comprehensive guide to books, articles, courses, and professional organizations that can support leaders in their ongoing development. By engaging with these resources, leaders can deepen their understanding of ethical principles, enhance their leadership skills, and stay informed about emerging trends and best practices.

Books on Ethical Leadership

Books provide in-depth insights and perspectives on ethical leadership, drawing from the experiences and research of experts in the field. The following books are highly recommended for leaders seeking to expand their knowledge and understanding of ethical leadership:

1. "Emotional Intelligence: Why It Can Matter More Than IQ" by Daniel Goleman

Goleman's seminal work on emotional intelligence explores the critical role of self-awareness, self-regulation, motivation, empathy, and social skills in effective leadership. The book highlights how emotional intelligence contributes to ethical decision-making and the development of strong, empathetic leadership.

2. "Primal Leadership: Realizing the Power of Emotional Intelligence" by Daniel Goleman, Richard Boyatzis, and Annie McKee

This book delves into the concept of resonant leadership, emphasizing the importance of emotional intelligence in creating a positive organizational climate. It provides practical strategies for leaders to develop their emotional intelligence and foster a culture of empathy and ethical behavior.

3. "The Responsible Company: What We've Learned from Patagonia's First 40 Years" by Yvon Chouinard and Vincent Stanley

Chouinard and Stanley share insights from Patagonia's journey as a socially responsible and ethical company. The book offers practical advice on integrating ethical principles into business practices and highlights the impact of ethical leadership on organizational success and sustainability.

4. "How Google Works" by Eric Schmidt and Jonathan Rosenberg

Schmidt and Rosenberg provide a behind-the-scenes look at Google's management practices, emphasizing the importance of innovation, collaboration, and ethical leadership. The book offers valuable lessons on creating an organizational culture that fosters trust, respect, and continuous improvement.

5. "Good Power: Leading Positive Change in Our Lives, Work, and World" by Ginni Rometty

In her book, Rometty discusses her experiences as the CEO of IBM and provides insights into ethical leadership and positive change. She emphasizes the importance of leading with integrity, empathy, and a commitment to social responsibility.

6. "Onward: How Starbucks Fought for Its Life without Losing Its Soul" by Howard Schultz and Joanne Gordon

Schultz's memoir recounts his return to Starbucks and the challenges he faced in revitalizing the company. The book highlights the role of ethical leadership in navigating crises and driving organizational success while maintaining core values.

7. "Creating Shared Value: How to Reinvent Capitalism—and Unleash a Wave of Innovation and Growth" by Michael E. Porter and Mark R. Kramer

Porter and Kramer introduce the concept of creating shared value, emphasizing the importance of aligning business practices with social and environmental goals. The book provides a framework for leaders to integrate ethical principles into their strategic vision and operations.

Articles and Journals

Articles and journals offer up-to-date research and insights on ethical leadership, providing a valuable resource for staying informed about emerging trends and best practices. The following journals and articles are recommended for further reading:

1. "Journal of Business Ethics"

The *Journal of Business Ethics* publishes high-quality research on various aspects of ethical leadership, corporate social responsibility, and organizational behavior. It is a valuable resource for leaders seeking to stay informed about the latest research and developments in the field.

2. "Harvard Business Review"

Harvard Business Review offers a wealth of articles on leadership, ethics, and management. Notable articles include "Strategy and Society: The Link Between Competitive Advantage and Corporate Social Responsibility" by Michael E. Porter and Mark R. Kramer, which explores the relationship between ethical leadership and business performance.

3. "Academy of Management Journal"

The *Academy of Management Journal* publishes empirical research on management and organizational behavior. Articles such as "Psychological Conditions of Personal Engagement and Disengagement at Work" by William A. Kahn provide valuable insights into the role of ethical leadership in fostering employee engagement and well-being.

4. "The Impact of Ethical Leadership on Employee Outcomes: The Roles of Psychological Empowerment and Ethical Climate" by Marylene Gagné et al.

This article, published in the *Journal of Business Ethics*, examines the relationship between ethical leadership, psychological empowerment, and ethical climate. It provides empirical evidence on the positive impact of ethical leadership on employee outcomes.

5. "Leading Change" by John P. Kotter

While not an article, Kotter's work on change management, published in *Harvard Business Review*, is essential reading for leaders seeking to drive ethical change within their organizations. Kotter's framework for leading change emphasizes the importance of vision, communication, and empowerment.

Online Courses and Certifications

Online courses and certifications provide flexible and accessible opportunities for leaders to develop their ethical leadership skills. The following courses and programs are recommended for professional development:

1. "Leading with Effective Communication (Inclusive Leadership Training)" by Catalyst

Offered by Catalyst, this course focuses on developing inclusive leadership skills, including effective communication, empathy, and ethical decision-making. It is available on Coursera and provides practical strategies for fostering an inclusive and ethical work environment.

2. "Ethical Leadership Through Giving Voice to Values" by University of Virginia

This course, available on Coursera, introduces the Giving Voice to Values (GVV) approach to ethical leadership. It emphasizes the importance of aligning actions with values and provides tools for addressing ethical dilemmas in the workplace.

3. "Business Ethics for the Real World" by University of Illinois at

Urbana-Champaign

Offered on Coursera, this course covers fundamental concepts in business ethics, including ethical decision-making, corporate social responsibility, and the role of ethics in leadership. It provides a solid foundation for understanding and practicing ethical leadership.

4. "Corporate Social Responsibility (CSR): A Strategic Approach" by University of London

This course, available on Coursera, explores the strategic aspects of CSR, including the integration of ethical principles into business practices. It provides practical insights for leaders seeking to drive social and environmental impact through ethical leadership.

5. "Leadership and Ethics: Moral Leadership in a Troubled World" by Yale University

Offered through Yale's Executive Education program, this course examines the role of moral leadership in addressing global challenges. It covers topics such as ethical decision-making, corporate governance, and social responsibility, providing leaders with the tools to navigate complex ethical issues.

Professional Organizations and Networks

Professional organizations and networks offer opportunities for leaders to connect with peers, share best practices, and stay informed about developments in ethical leadership. The following organizations are recommended for leaders seeking to expand their professional network:

1. Business Roundtable Institute for Corporate Ethics

The Business Roundtable Institute for Corporate Ethics brings together business leaders, scholars, and policymakers to advance ethical leadership and corporate responsibility. The institute offers resources, research, and networking opportunities for leaders committed to ethical practices.

2. Ethics & Compliance Initiative (ECI)

The Ethics & Compliance Initiative is a membership organization that provides resources, training, and certification programs for ethics and compliance professionals. ECI offers a platform for leaders to share insights, collaborate, and stay informed about best practices in ethical leadership.

3. Society for Human Resource Management (SHRM)

SHRM is a professional association that offers resources, certification programs, and networking opportunities for HR professionals. SHRM's focus on ethical leadership and organizational culture makes it a valuable resource for leaders seeking to foster a positive and ethical work environment.

4. International Leadership Association (ILA)

The International Leadership Association is a global network of leadership scholars, practitioners, and educators. ILA offers conferences, publications, and resources that explore various aspects of leadership, including ethics and social responsibility.

5. Net Impact

Net Impact is a global community of students and professionals who seek to drive social and environmental change through business. The organization offers resources, events, and networking opportunities for leaders committed to ethical leadership and sustainability.

Conclusion

The journey of ethical leadership is one of continuous learning, reflection, and growth. By engaging with the resources for further reading and professional development outlined in this chapter, leaders can deepen their understanding of ethical principles, enhance their leadership skills, and stay informed about emerging trends and best practices.

Books, articles, online courses, and professional organizations provide valuable insights and opportunities for leaders to develop their ethical leadership capabilities. By prioritizing continuous learning and professional development, leaders can ensure that they are equipped to navigate the complexities of the modern business environment with integrity, empathy, and fairness.

The principles of the Golden Rule—treating others as you would like to be treated—serve as a guiding framework for ethical leadership. By embracing these principles and committing to ongoing development, leaders can create a positive and lasting impact on their organizations and the broader community.

References

Brenner, S. N. (2009). Johnson & Johnson's Credo: A corporate cultural relic or a practical guide to employees. *Journal of Business Ethics, 85*(3), 219-223.

Chouinard, Y., & Stanley, V. (2023). *The future of the responsible company: What we've learned from Patagonia's first 50 Years*. Patagonia.

Harvard Business School. (2020). *MBA program*. Retrieved from https://www.hbs.edu/mba/

Peters, J. (2019). *Employee engagement: Creating high positive energy at work*. Knowledge Resources.

Kaplan, R. S., & Norton, D. P. (1996). *The balanced scorecard: Translating strategy into action*. Harvard Business School Press.

Lepsinger, R., & Lucia, A. D. (1997). *The art and science of 360-degree feedback*. Pfeiffer.

Nadella, S. (2017). *Hit refresh: The quest to rediscover Microsoft's soul and imagine a better future for everyone*. Harper Business.

Parasuraman, A., Zeithaml, V. A., & Berry, L. L. (1985). A conceptual model of service quality and its implications for future research. *Journal of Marketing, 49*(4), 41-50.

Porter, M. E., & Kramer, M. R. (2006). Strategy and society: The link between competitive advantage and corporate social responsibility. *Harvard Business Review, 84*(12), 78-92.

Rometty, G. (2019). *Good power: Leading positive change in our lives, work, and world*. Harvard Business Review Press.

Schmidt, E., & Rosenberg, J. (2014). *How Google works*. Grand Central Publishing.

Sims, R. R. (1992). The challenge of ethical behavior in organizations. *Journal of Business Ethics, 11*(7), 505-513.

Stein, S. (2023). *Emotional intelligence*. Wiley Publishing, Inc.

Chapter 17

The Legacy of Ethical Leadership

As we reach the conclusion of this exploration into ethical leadership, it is essential to reflect on the journey we have undertaken and the profound impact that ethical leadership can have on organizations and society. Ethical leadership, guided by the Golden Rule—treating others as you would like to be treated—serves as a beacon for navigating the complexities of modern organizational life with integrity, empathy, and fairness. This principle is timeless, transcending cultural and organizational boundaries, and its application is more critical than ever in today's dynamic and interconnected world.

The Enduring Importance of Ethical Leadership

Ethical leadership is not merely about adhering to laws and regulations; it encompasses a commitment to integrity, fairness, empathy, and a deep sense of responsibility toward all stakeholders. At its core, ethical leadership is about doing the right thing, even when it is difficult or inconvenient. This commitment to ethical behavior fosters trust, enhances employee engagement, and builds a positive reputation, all of which contribute to the organization's overall success and sustainability.

Throughout this book, we have delved into the foundational principles of ethical leadership, explored practical strategies for applying these principles in various contexts, and examined real-world case studies that illustrate the transformative power of ethical leadership. We have seen how leaders can foster trust, build strong teams, drive innovation, and create sustainable success by adhering to the principles of the Golden Rule.

Foundations of Ethical Leadership

In the **Foundations of Ethical Leadership** (Part 1), we established the essential principles that underpin ethical leadership. We explored the concept of the Golden Rule across different cultures and religions, highlighting its universal applicability and relevance. We also discussed the core principles of integrity, fairness, accountability, and empathy, providing a robust framework for ethical leadership (Hofstede, 1991; Stein, 2023).

Applying the Golden Rule in Leadership Practices

Moving to **Part 2: Applying the Golden Rule in Leadership Practices**, we provided practical insights and strategies for integrating the Golden Rule into various aspects of leadership. We examined how leaders can enhance employee engagement and productivity, resolve conflicts ethically, and adapt their leadership styles to different situations while maintaining a commitment to ethical behavior (Schmidt & Rosenberg, 2014; Schultz & Yang, 2011).

Cultivating a Sustainable and Ethical Organizational Culture

Part 3: Cultivating a Sustainable and Ethical Organizational Culture emphasized the importance of creating an environment where ethical behavior is valued and encouraged. We explored strategies for building a respectful organizational culture, promoting diversity and inclusion, and fostering a culture of trust and accountability. These elements are crucial for long-term organizational success and sustainability (Chouinard & Stanley, 2022; Nadella, 2017).

Leadership in Action: Case Studies and Best Practices

In **Part 4: Leadership in Action: Case Studies and Best Practices**, we analyzed real-world examples of organizations that have successfully implemented ethical leadership practices. These case studies provided concrete evidence of the positive impact of ethical leadership on organizational performance and reputation. We also identified best practices that leaders can adopt to foster ethical behavior and drive sustainable success (Brenner, 2009; Chesky, 2020).

The Future of Ethical Leadership

Part 5: The Future of Ethical Leadership looked towards the future, exploring emerging trends and challenges that will shape the landscape of ethical leadership. We discussed the impact of globalization, technological advancements, and societal shifts on leadership practices. We also highlighted the importance of sustainability, resilience, and continuous learning in preparing leaders to navigate future challenges with integrity and compassion (Earley & Ang, 2003; Schmidt & Rosenberg, 2014).

Resources for Further Reading and Professional Development

In **Chapter 16: Resources for Further Reading and Professional Development**, we provided a comprehensive guide to books, articles, courses, and professional organizations that can support leaders in their ongoing development. By engaging with these resources, leaders can deepen their understanding of ethical principles, enhance their leadership skills, and stay informed about emerging trends and best practices.

The Impact of Ethical Leadership on Organizational Success

Ethical leadership has a profound impact on various aspects of organizational success, including employee engagement, customer satisfaction, financial performance, and social responsibility. By fostering a culture of integrity, fairness, and empathy, ethical leaders can drive sustainable success and create a positive legacy.

Employee Engagement

Ethical leadership enhances employee engagement by creating a supportive and respectful work environment. Engaged employees are more likely to be committed to the organization's goals and values, leading to higher levels of productivity and job satisfaction. Leaders who prioritize ethical behavior and treat employees with respect and fairness foster a culture of trust and collaboration, which contributes to employee well-being and retention (Peters, 2019; Allen & Meyer, 1990).

Customer Satisfaction

Customers are increasingly valuing ethical behavior and social responsibility in the organizations they support. Ethical leadership enhances customer satisfaction by building trust and demonstrating a commitment to ethical practices. Organizations that prioritize ethical behavior and transparency can foster customer loyalty and differentiate themselves in the market (Parasuraman, Zeithaml, & Berry, 1985).

Financial Performance

There is a strong link between ethical leadership and financial performance. Organizations that prioritize ethical behavior are more likely to achieve sustainable financial success by building a positive reputation, fostering customer loyalty, and enhancing employee engagement. Ethical leadership also helps mitigate risks associated with unethical behavior, such as legal issues and reputational damage (Porter & Kramer, 2006).

Social Responsibility

Ethical leadership extends beyond the organization to impact society at large. Leaders who prioritize social responsibility and ethical behavior can drive positive change in their communities and contribute to broader social and environmental goals. By aligning business practices with social and environmental values, organizations can create shared value and enhance their long-term sustainability (Porter & Kramer, 2011).

The Role of Continuous Learning and Development

The journey of ethical leadership is one of continuous learning, reflection, and growth. Leaders must prioritize their ongoing development to stay informed about emerging trends, enhance their leadership skills, and deepen their understanding of ethical principles. By engaging with resources for further reading and professional development, leaders can ensure that they are equipped to navigate the complexities of the modern business environment with integrity, empathy, and fairness.

Professional Development Programs

Professional development programs provide structured opportunities for leaders to enhance their ethical leadership skills. These programs often include courses, workshops, and seminars on topics such as ethical decision-making, corporate social responsibility, and emotional intelligence. By participating in these programs, leaders can stay informed about best practices and emerging trends in ethical leadership (Harvard Business School, 2020).

Mentorship and Networking

Mentorship and networking are critical components of ethical leadership development. Experienced leaders can provide guidance, support, and inspiration to emerging leaders, helping them internalize ethical principles and practices. Networking with peers and experts in the field also provides opportunities for collaboration, sharing best practices, and staying informed about developments in ethical leadership (Stein, 2023).

Reflective Practices

Reflective practices, such as self-assessments, journaling, and feedback, are essential for continuous learning and growth. By engaging in self-reflection, leaders can assess their values, behaviors, and decisions, identify areas for improvement, and commit to ethical principles. Regular feedback and evaluation also provide valuable insights into how well ethical principles are being integrated and highlight areas for further development (Schmidt & Rosenberg, 2014).

The Legacy of Ethical Leadership

The legacy of ethical leadership is built on the principles of integrity, fairness, empathy, and a deep sense of responsibility toward all stakeholders. By embracing these principles and committing to ongoing development, leaders can create a positive and lasting impact on their organizations and the broader community.

Creating a Positive Organizational Culture

Ethical leadership plays a crucial role in shaping organizational culture. By modeling ethical behavior and fostering a culture of trust, respect, and collaboration, leaders can create a positive work environment where employees feel valued and motivated. This positive culture contributes to employee engagement, customer satisfaction, and overall organizational success (Nadella, 2017).

Driving Sustainable Success

Ethical leadership is essential for achieving sustainable success. By prioritizing ethical behavior and social responsibility, leaders can build a positive reputation, foster customer loyalty, and enhance financial performance. Ethical leadership also helps organizations navigate challenges and uncertainties with integrity and resilience, ensuring long-term sustainability (Chouinard & Stanley, 2022).

Contributing to Social and Environmental Goals

Ethical leadership extends beyond the organization to impact society at large. Leaders who prioritize social responsibility and ethical behavior can drive positive change in their communities and contribute to broader social and environmental goals. By aligning business practices with social and environmental values, organizations can create shared value and enhance their long-term sustainability (Porter & Kramer, 2011).

Conclusion

As we conclude this exploration of ethical leadership, it is clear that the principles of the Golden Rule—treating others as you would like to be treated—are more relevant and essential than ever. Ethical leadership is not just a theoretical ideal but a practical imperative that can drive meaningful change and success in organizations.

By fostering a culture of integrity, fairness, empathy, and accountability, ethical leaders can enhance employee engagement, customer satisfaction, and financial performance. They can also contribute to broader social and environmental goals, creating a positive and lasting impact on their organizations and communities.

The journey of ethical leadership is one of continuous learning, reflection, and growth. By engaging with resources for further reading and professional development, leaders can deepen their understanding of ethical principles, enhance their leadership skills, and stay informed about emerging trends and best practices.

As organizations navigate the complexities of the modern business environment, the commitment to ethical leadership and the principles of the Golden Rule will remain essential for sustainable success and positive social responsibility. By embracing these principles and leading with integrity, empathy, and fairness, leaders can create a legacy of ethical behavior and sustainable success that will endure for generations to come.

References

Allen, N. J., & Meyer, J. P. (1990). The measurement and antecedents of affective, continuance and normative commitment to the organization.

Journal of Occupational Psychology, 63(1), 1-18.

Brenner, S. N. (2009). Johnson & Johnson's Credo: A corporate cultural relic or a practical guide to employees. *Journal of Business Ethics, 85*(3), 219-223.

Chouinard, Y., & Stanley, V. (2023). *The future of the responsible company: What we've learned from Patagonia's first 50 Years.* Patagonia.

Earley, P. C., & Ang, S. (2003). *Cultural intelligence: Individual interactions across cultures.* Stanford University Press.

Harvard Business School. (2020). *MBA program.* Retrieved from https://www.hbs.edu/mba/

Hofstede, G. (1991). *Cultures and organizations: Software of the mind.* McGraw-Hill.

Peters, J. (2019). *Employee engagement: Creating high positive energy at work.* Knowledge Resources.

Nadella, S. (2017). *Hit refresh: The quest to rediscover Microsoft's soul and imagine a better future for everyone.* Harper Business.

Parasuraman, A., Zeithaml, V. A., & Berry, L. L. (1985). A conceptual model of service quality and its implications for future research. *Journal of Marketing, 49*(4), 41-50.

Porter, M. E., & Kramer, M. R. (2006). Strategy and society: The link between competitive advantage and corporate social responsibility. *Harvard Business Review, 84*(12), 78-92.

Porter, M. E., & Kramer, M. R. (2011). Creating shared value. *Harvard Business Review, 89*(1/2), 62-77.

Schmidt, E., & Rosenberg, J. (2014). *How Google works.* Grand Central Publishing.

Schultz, H., & Yang, D. J. (2011). *Onward: How Starbucks fought for its life without losing its soul.* Rodale Books.

Stein, S. (2023). *Emotional intelligence.* Wiley Publishing, Inc. .

Appendices

The following appendices are designed to provide practical tools, resources, and additional information to support the concepts and strategies discussed throughout this book on ethical leadership. These appendices offer readers opportunities to deepen their understanding, apply ethical principles in real-world scenarios, and enhance their leadership skills. Whether you are a seasoned leader or an emerging professional, these resources will help you navigate the complexities of ethical leadership with confidence and integrity.

Each appendix serves a specific purpose, from self-assessment tools and case studies to practical frameworks and further reading recommendations. By engaging with these materials, you can reflect on your own practices, learn from exemplary cases, and access resources that support continuous professional development. We encourage you to explore these appendices and integrate the insights and tools into your leadership journey.

Appendix A

Ethical Leadership Self-Assessment

Purpose: This self-assessment tool allows leaders to evaluate their ethical behavior and identify areas for improvement. It encourages self-awareness and personal growth by reflecting on key ethical leadership principles such as integrity, empathy, fairness, and accountability.

Instructions: Read each statement carefully and rate your agreement using the following scale:

- 1: Strongly Disagree

- 2: Disagree

- 3: Neutral

- 4: Agree

- 5: Strongly Agree

Self-Assessment Statements

Integrity

I consistently demonstrate honesty in my interactions with others.

I uphold ethical standards, even when it is challenging or inconvenient.

I take responsibility for my actions and their consequences.

I ensure that my decisions align with the organization's values and ethical principles.

Empathy

I actively listen to the concerns and perspectives of others.

I demonstrate compassion and understanding towards colleagues and employees.

I consider the impact of my decisions on the well-being of others.

I foster a supportive and inclusive environment for all team members.

Fairness

I treat all employees and colleagues with fairness and respect.

I ensure that decisions and policies are applied consistently and equitably.

I avoid favoritism and ensure equal opportunities for all team members.

I address conflicts and disputes impartially and justly.

Accountability

I hold myself accountable for upholding ethical standards.

I encourage transparency and openness in organizational practices.

I create mechanisms for reporting and addressing unethical behavior.

I provide constructive feedback and hold others accountable for their actions.

Scoring

Add up your scores for each section: Integrity, Empathy, Fairness, and Accountability.

Total Score: _____ (Maximum possible score: 80)

Interpretation

Score: 64-80 (High Ethical Leadership) You demonstrate strong ethical leadership qualities. Continue to uphold these standards and serve as a role model for others.

Score: 48-63 (Moderate Ethical Leadership) You have a solid foundation in ethical leadership but may benefit from further development in specific areas. Identify opportunities for growth and seek feedback to enhance your skills.

Score: Below 48 (Needs Improvement) There are significant areas for improvement in your ethical leadership. Reflect on the specific statements where you scored lower and develop a plan to address these gaps.

Reflective Questions

Which areas did you score the highest in? What behaviors contribute to these strengths?

Which areas did you score the lowest in? What steps can you take to improve in these areas?

How can you apply the principles of the Golden Rule—treating others as you would like to be treated—to enhance your ethical leadership?

What specific actions can you take to foster a culture of integrity, empathy, fairness, and accountability within your organization?

Further Reading

For additional insights into ethical leadership and personal development, consider the following resources:

Goleman, D., & Lenz, M. (2020). *Emotionally intelligent leader Daniel Goleman*. Findaway World.

Chouinard, Y., & Stanley, V. (2023). *The future of the responsible company: What we've learned from Patagonia's first 50 Years*. Patagonia.

Nadella, S. (2017). *Hit refresh: The quest to rediscover Microsoft's soul and imagine a better future for everyone*. Harper Business.

Schmidt, E., & Rosenberg, J. (2014). *How Google works*. Grand Central Publishing.

Stein, S. (2023). *Emotional intelligence*. Wiley Publishing, Inc.

References

Chouinard, Y., & Stanley, V. (2023). *The future of the responsible company: What we've learned from Patagonia's first 50 Years*. Patagonia.

Goleman, D., & Lenz, M. (2020). *Emotionally intelligent leader Daniel Goleman*. Findaway World.

Nadella, S. (2017). *Hit refresh: The quest to rediscover Microsoft's soul and imagine a better future for everyone*. Harper Business.

Schmidt, E., & Rosenberg, J. (2014). *How Google works*. Grand Central Publishing.

Stein, S. (2023). *Emotional intelligence*. Wiley Publishing, Inc.

Appendix B

Case Studies

Purpose: Provide detailed examples of ethical leadership in action across different industries and contexts. These case studies offer valuable insights and lessons that can be applied to various organizational settings.

Case Study 1: Johnson & Johnson's Tylenol Crisis

Background: In 1982, Johnson & Johnson faced a major crisis when cyanide-laced Tylenol capsules resulted in several deaths.

Ethical Leadership in Action:

Transparency and Communication: The company immediately informed the public and authorities about the crisis.

Responsibility: Johnson & Johnson recalled all Tylenol products from the shelves, demonstrating a commitment to customer safety over profit.

Outcome: The company's swift and ethical response helped rebuild trust with the public and maintained its reputation for integrity.

Case Study 2: Patagonia's Environmental Responsibility

Background: Patagonia is known for its commitment to environmental sustainability.

Ethical Leadership in Action:

Sustainable Practices: The company implements eco-friendly practices in its supply chain and product manufacturing.

Transparency: Patagonia openly shares its environmental impact and encourages other companies to adopt sustainable practices.

Outcome: Patagonia's ethical leadership has enhanced its brand reputation and customer loyalty, contributing to its long-term success.

Case Study 3: Google's Organizational Culture

Background: Google is renowned for its innovative and inclusive organizational culture.

Ethical Leadership in Action:

Inclusivity: Google promotes diversity and inclusion through various programs and policies.

Employee Well-Being: The company provides extensive benefits and support for employee well-being and development.

Outcome: Google's ethical leadership has fostered a highly engaged and productive workforce, driving innovation and growth.

Questions for Discussion

What ethical principles were demonstrated in each case study?

How did the leaders' actions align with the Golden Rule?

What lessons can be applied to your own leadership context?

References

Brenner, S. N. (2009). Johnson & Johnson's Credo: A corporate cultural relic or a practical guide to employees. *Journal of Business Ethics, 85*(3), 219-223.

Chouinard, Y., & Stanley, V. (2023). *The future of the responsible company: What we've learned from Patagonia's first 50 Years.* Patagonia.

Schmidt, E., & Rosenberg, J. (2014). *How Google works.* Grand Central Publishing.

Appendix C

Ethical Decision-Making Framework

Purpose: Offer a practical framework for making ethical decisions in complex situations. This framework helps leaders navigate ethical dilemmas and make decisions that align with organizational values and principles.

Step-by-Step Ethical Decision-Making Framework

Identify the Ethical Dilemma:

Clearly define the ethical issue or dilemma.

Identify the stakeholders involved and the potential impact on each.

Gather Information:

Collect relevant information, including facts, laws, policies, and stakeholder perspectives.

Ensure the information is accurate and comprehensive.

Evaluate Options:

Generate a list of possible actions or solutions.

Consider the ethical implications of each option.

Apply Ethical Principles:

Use ethical principles such as the Golden Rule, integrity, fairness, and empathy to evaluate each option.

Consider how each option aligns with the organization's values and ethical standards.

Make a Decision:

Choose the option that best aligns with ethical principles and organizational values.

Ensure the decision is fair, transparent, and justifiable.

Implement the Decision:

Communicate the decision clearly to all stakeholders.

Take necessary actions to implement the decision effectively.

Evaluate the Outcome:

Assess the impact of the decision on stakeholders and the organization.

Reflect on lessons learned and areas for improvement.

Example Scenario

Scenario: A manager discovers that a popular product has a design flaw that could potentially harm customers.

Application of the Framework:

Identify the Ethical Dilemma: The dilemma is whether to recall the product, which could be costly or to continue selling it, risking customer safety.

Gather Information: Collect data on the extent of the flaw, potential risks, customer feedback, and regulatory requirements.

Evaluate Options: Options include recalling the product, fixing the flaw, issuing a statement, or continuing sales without disclosure.

Apply Ethical Principles: The Golden Rule and integrity suggest prioritizing customer safety by recalling the product.

Make a Decision: Decide to recall the product and communicate the issue transparently to customers.

Implement the Decision: Announce the recall, provide instructions for returns, and address the flaw.

Evaluate the Outcome: Monitor customer responses and financial impact and ensure similar issues are prevented in the future.

References

Kaplan, R. S., & Norton, D. P. (1996). *The balanced scorecard: Translating strategy into action*. Harvard Business School Press.

Sims, R. R. (1992). The challenge of ethical behavior in organizations. *Journal of Business Ethics, 11*(7), 505-513.

Appendix D

Resources for Further Learning

Purpose: Provide readers with additional resources to deepen their understanding of ethical leadership.

Recommended Books

Goleman, D., & Lenz, M. (2020). *Emotionally intelligent leader Daniel Goleman*. Findaway World.

Chouinard, Y., & Stanley, V. (2023). *The future of the responsible company: What we've learned from Patagonia's first 50 Years*. Patagonia.

Nadella, S. (2017). *Hit refresh: The quest to rediscover Microsoft's soul and imagine a better future for everyone*. Harper Business.

Schmidt, E., & Rosenberg, J. (2014). *How Google works*. Grand Central Publishing.

Stein, S. (2023). *Emotional intelligence.* Wiley Publishing, Inc. .

Recommended Articles and Journals

Journal of Business Ethics: A leading journal publishing research on various aspects of ethical leadership.

Harvard Business Review: Offers articles on leadership, ethics, and management. Notable articles include "Strategy and Society: The Link Between Competitive Advantage and Corporate Social Responsibility" by Michael E. Porter and Mark R. Kramer.

Academy of Management Journal: Publishes empirical research on management and organizational behavior. Articles such as "Psychological Conditions of Personal Engagement and Disengagement at Work" by

William A. Kahn provide valuable insights into ethical leadership.

Online Courses and Certifications

"Leading with Effective Communication (Inclusive Leadership Training)" by Catalyst: Available on Coursera, this course focuses on developing inclusive leadership skills.

"Ethical Leadership Through Giving Voice to Values" by the University of Virginia: Available on Coursera, this course introduces the Giving Voice to Values approach to ethical leadership.

"Business Ethics for the Real World" by University of Illinois at Urbana-Champaign: Available on Coursera, this course covers fundamental concepts in business ethics.

"Corporate Social Responsibility (CSR): A Strategic Approach" by the University of London: Available on Coursera, this course explores the strategic aspects of CSR.

"Leadership and Ethics: Moral Leadership in a Troubled World" by Yale University: Offered through Yale's Executive Education program, this course examines the role of moral leadership.

Professional Organizations and Networks

Business Roundtable Institute for Corporate Ethics: Brings together business leaders, scholars, and policymakers to advance ethical leadership.

Ethics & Compliance Initiative (ECI): Provides resources, training, and certification programs for ethics and compliance professionals.

Society for Human Resource Management (SHRM): Offers resources, certification programs, and networking opportunities for HR professionals.

International Leadership Association (ILA): A global network of leadership scholars, practitioners, and educators.

Net Impact: A global community of students and professionals who seek to drive social and environmental change through business.

References

Goleman, D., & Lenz, M. (2020). *Emotionally intelligent leader Daniel Goleman.* Findaway World.

Nadella, S. (2017). *Hit refresh: The quest to rediscover Microsoft's soul and imagine a better future for everyone.* Harper Business.

Porter, M. E., & Kramer, M. R. (2006). Strategy and society: The link between competitive advantage and corporate social responsibility. *Harvard Business Review, 84*(12), 78-92.

Schmidt, E., & Rosenberg, J. (2014). *How Google works.* Grand Central Publishing.

Stein, S. (2023). *Emotional intelligence.* Wiley Publishing, Inc. .

Appendix E

Sample Ethical Policies and Codes of Conduct

Purpose: Provide examples of ethical policies and codes of conduct that organizations can adopt or adapt to foster a culture of integrity and accountability.

Sample Code of Conduct

Introduction This Code of Conduct outlines the ethical standards and principles that guide our behavior and decision-making processes. All employees, leaders, and board members are expected to adhere to these standards to maintain a culture of integrity, fairness, and respect.

Core Values

Integrity: We act with honesty and uphold the highest standards of moral and ethical values.

Respect: We treat all individuals with dignity and respect, fostering an inclusive and collaborative environment.

Accountability: We take responsibility for our actions and their impact on others.

Transparency: We conduct our business with openness and transparency.

Conflicts of Interest Employees must avoid situations where their personal interests could conflict with the interests of the organization. Any potential conflicts must be disclosed to the relevant authority.

Confidentiality Employees must maintain the confidentiality of sensitive information and use it only for legitimate business purposes. Unauthorized disclosure of confidential information is prohibited.

Fair Dealing We are committed to fair and ethical dealings with our customers, suppliers, and competitors. We do not engage in practices that could harm our reputation or the trust of our stakeholders.

Reporting Violations Employees are encouraged to report any violations of this Code of Conduct or any unethical behavior. Reports can be made confidentially through our whistleblower hotline.

Compliance Failure to comply with this Code of Conduct may result in disciplinary action, up to and including termination of employment.

Sample Ethical Policies

Conflict of Interest Policy Employees must disclose any potential conflicts of interest and avoid situations where their personal interests could influence their professional decisions. Regular training on conflict of interest policies will be provided.

Whistleblower Policy: We are committed to maintaining an open and supportive environment where employees can report unethical behavior without fear of retaliation. All reports will be investigated thoroughly and confidentially.

Corporate Social Responsibility Policy We are dedicated to conducting our business in a socially responsible manner. This includes minimizing our environmental impact, supporting community initiatives, and ensuring fair labor practices in our supply chain.

Diversity and Inclusion Policy We value diversity and strive to create an inclusive workplace where all employees feel respected and valued. We are committed to equal opportunity and will provide training to promote diversity and inclusion.

Guidelines for Developing Ethical Policies

Align with Core Values: Ensure that all policies reflect the organization's core values and ethical principles.

Clear Communication: Communicate policies clearly to all employees and provide regular training to reinforce understanding.

Consistent Enforcement: Apply policies consistently and fairly across the organization to maintain trust and credibility.

Regular Review: Periodically review and update policies to ensure they remain relevant and effective.

References

Brenner, S. N. (2009). Johnson & Johnson's Credo: A corporate cultural relic or a practical guide to employees. *Journal of Business Ethics, 85*(3), 219-223.

Nadella, S. (2017). *Hit refresh: The quest to rediscover Microsoft's soul and imagine a better future for everyone*. Harper Business.

Stein, S. (2023). *Emotional intelligence*. Wiley Publishing, Inc. .

Appendix F

Workshop and Training Materials

Purpose: Offer materials for conducting workshops and training sessions on ethical leadership. These resources provide a practical approach to fostering ethical behavior and developing leadership skills.

Sample Workshop Agenda

Title: Ethical Leadership Workshop

Duration: 1 Day

Agenda:

9:00 AM - 9:30 AM: Welcome and Introduction

Overview of the workshop objectives

Introduction to Ethical Leadership

9:30 AM - 10:30 AM: Understanding Ethical Principles

Presentation on core ethical principles (integrity, empathy, fairness, accountability)

Group discussion and Q&A

10:30 AM - 10:45 AM: Break

10:45 AM - 12:00 PM: Ethical Decision-Making Framework

Introduction to the ethical decision-making framework

Interactive case study analysis

12:00 PM - 1:00 PM: Lunch Break

1:00 PM - 2:30 PM: Developing Emotional Intelligence

Presentation on the role of emotional intelligence in ethical leadership

Group activities and role-playing exercises
2:30 PM - 2:45 PM: Break

2:45 PM - 4:00 PM: Building an Ethical Organizational Culture

Strategies for fostering an ethical culture

Group discussion and action planning
4:00 PM - 4:30 PM: Wrap-Up and Reflection

Summary of key takeaways

Reflective questions and feedback

Activities and Exercises

Activity 1: Ethical Dilemma Role-Playing

Objective: To practice ethical decision-making in a safe environment.

Instructions: Divide participants into small groups. Provide each group with a scenario involving an ethical dilemma. Ask them to discuss and role-play their response, considering the ethical principles discussed.

Discussion: After the role-playing, reconvene and discuss the different approaches and their ethical implications.

Activity 2: Emotional Intelligence Self-Assessment

Objective: To increase self-awareness and identify areas for development.

Instructions: Distribute the emotional intelligence self-assessment questionnaire. Ask participants to complete the assessment individually.

Discussion: Facilitate a discussion on the importance of emotional intelligence in ethical leadership and strategies for improvement.

Facilitator Guides and Handouts
Facilitator Guide: Ethical Decision-Making Framework

Introduction: Overview of the ethical decision-making framework.

Step-by-Step Instructions: Detailed instructions for each step of the framework.

Discussion Points: Key discussion points and questions to facilitate understanding.

Handout: Ethical Leadership Principles

Overview: Summary of core ethical principles (integrity, empathy, fairness, accountability).

Examples: Real-world examples of ethical leadership in action.

Reflection Questions: Questions to encourage self-reflection and application of principles.

References

Goleman, D., & Lenz, M. (2020). *Emotionally intelligent leader Daniel Goleman.* Findaway World.

Nadella, S. (2017). *Hit refresh: The quest to rediscover Microsoft's soul and imagine a better future for everyone.* Harper Business.

Schmidt, E., & Rosenberg, J. (2014). *How Google works.* Grand Central Publishing.

Stein, S. (2023). *Emotional intelligence.* Wiley Publishing, Inc.

Appendix G

Key Definitions and Concepts

Purpose: Clarify key terms and concepts related to ethical leadership. This appendix serves as a quick reference for readers to understand important terminology.

Key Definitions

Ethics: A set of moral principles that govern an individual's behavior and decision-making.

Integrity: The quality of being honest and having strong moral principles.

Empathy: The ability to understand and share the feelings of others.

Fairness: The quality of making judgments that are free from discrimination and bias.

Accountability: The obligation to explain, justify, and take responsibility for one's actions.

Corporate Social Responsibility (CSR): A business approach that contributes to sustainable development by delivering economic, social, and environmental benefits for all stakeholders.

Emotional Intelligence (EI): The ability to recognize, understand, and manage one's own emotions and to recognize, understand, and influence the emotions of others.

Transparency: The practice of being open, honest, and straightforward about company operations.

Stakeholder: Any individual or group that is affected by or can affect the activities of an organization.

Key Concepts

Golden Rule: Treat others as you would like to be treated. This principle is fundamental to ethical behavior and decision-making.

Ethical Decision-Making Framework: A structured approach to making decisions that align with ethical principles and organizational values.

Inclusive Leadership: A leadership style that values diversity, promotes equality, and fosters a sense of belonging for all team members.

Whistleblowing: The act of reporting unethical or illegal activities within an organization.

Conflict of Interest: A situation in which an individual's personal interests could potentially influence their professional decisions.

Visual Aids

Ethical Decision-Making Framework Diagram

A visual representation of the steps involved in the ethical decision-making process.

Emotional Intelligence Model

A diagram illustrating the components of emotional intelligence: self-awareness, self-regulation, motivation, empathy, and social skills.

References

Kaplan, R. S., & Norton, D. P. (1996). *The balanced scorecard: Translating strategy into action.* Harvard Business School Press.

Nadella, S. (2017). *Hit refresh: The quest to rediscover Microsoft's soul and imagine a better future for everyone.* Harper Business.

Porter, M. E., & Kramer, M. R. (2006). Strategy and society: The link between competitive advantage and corporate social responsibility. *Harvard Business Review, 84*(12), 78-92.

Stein, S. (2023). *Emotional intelligence.* Wiley Publishing, Inc.

Appendix H

Contact Information for Professional Support

Purpose: Provide contact information for professional organizations, consultants, and resources that can support ethical leadership development.

Professional Organizations

Business Roundtable Institute for Corporate Ethics

Website: www.corporate-ethics.org

Contact Information: info@corporate-ethics.org

Ethics & Compliance Initiative (ECI)

Website: www.ethics.org

Contact Information: membership@ethics.org

Society for Human Resource Management (SHRM)

Website: www.shrm.org

Contact Information: membership@shrm.org

International Leadership Association (ILA)

Website: www.ila-net.org

Contact Information: membership@ila-net.org

Net Impact

Website: www.netimpact.org

Contact Information: info@netimpact.org

Consultants and Firms

Ethical Leadership Group

Website: www.ethicalleadershipgroup.com

Contact Information: contact@ethicalleadershipgroup.com

Global Ethics Solutions

Website: www.globalethicssolutions.com

Contact Information: info@globalethicssolutions.com

Ethics Resource Center

Website: www.ethics.org

Contact Information: services@ethics.org

Legal and Ethical Advice

American Bar Association (ABA) Center for Professional Responsibility

Website: www.americanbar.org/groups/professional_responsibility.html

Contact Information: cpr@americanbar.org

Institute for Global Ethics

Website: www.globalethics.org

Contact Information: info@globalethics.org

References

Nadella, S. (2017). *Hit refresh: The quest to rediscover Microsoft's soul and imagine a better future for everyone.* Harper Business.

Porter, M. E., & Kramer, M. R. (2006). Strategy and society: The link between competitive advantage and corporate social responsibility. *Harvard Business Review, 84*(12), 78-92.

Schmidt, E., & Rosenberg, J. (2014). *How Google works*. Grand Central Publishing. Stein, S. (2023). *Emotional intelligence*. Wiley Publishing, Inc.